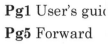

Prayer for your Job

Prayer for deliverance from curses

Develop Identity in Christ

Sozo English prayerbook
@ 2015 Sozo Ministries
All rights reserved.
www.sozotnt.org

Paperback: 346 pages
Publisher: Sozo Ministries
Language: English
ISBN-10: 0984219625
ISBN-13: 978-0984219629

Author(s): Tina Yu Chong, Tony Chong
Cover design: Christine Chong
email: sozoministries@gmail.com

Some notes about using this booklet

This prayer book was originally designed and wrote to help Christians of Chinese and East Asian cultural background. It is to help them walk with the Lord God daily, and to renew their mind, and also to set them free from the pagan worship. The book contents of blessings and promises of the Father God, as well as prayers to help believers to confess and repent all their sins and the bondages involved before they know Jesus. Also the contents help to fight spiritual battle in their daily walk with Jesus.

Please do not use all these prayers like a formula. Please pray with your heart, come before the Lord to confess and repent humbly and honestly. Surrender yourself totally to Him, and ask the Lord to help us to receive the Father's grace that has been given to us by the finished work of Jesus Christ. But the hour is coming, and is now here, when the true worshipers will worship the Father in spirit and truth, for the Father is seeking such people to worship Him. (John 4:23) Father God knows our heart, He knows our thoughts from afar, even the hidden thoughts that we know not. Come before him honestly, asking help from the Lord to surrender our entire being, and let Him work on us. For the word of God is living and active, sharper than

1

any two-edged sword, piercing to the division of soul and of spirit, of joints and of marrow, and discerning the thoughts and intentions of the heart. (Hebrew 4:12).

If you have any uncomfortable feelings during the prayer, like tight chest, yawning, oppression, heaviness, coughing, sleepiness, do not be afraid. You can pray in tongues, or ask the Lord to reveal the root cause, any foothold, and then deal with it. If anyone needs help and find it difficult to read out loud or can't finish it, he/ she will need someone beside him/her to encourage him/her to push through, or to intercede for the person, so that he/she can complete the prayer. If any manifestation happens during prayer, do not panic, do not focus on symptoms, complete the prayer to remove all the rights enemy gained from previous sin.

We suggest to always start with the Lordship prayer, we also suggest to put your name into the prayer to replace *"I"*, due to the fact that most of us received our salvation after we have grown up. We need to give every part of ourselves to the Lord. Using our name can help every part of us to identify with our name.

When you do the *"prayer for the restoration of Human Spirit"* just surrender all of yourself to the Lord, let Jesus reign in our spirit, soul, and body, let the spirit of the Lord work on us.

2

When you do the prayer of *"Prayer to Put on God's Full Armor"*, do meditate on the meaning of full armor, (you can also do the prophetic act of putting the full armor). We suggest you *"prayer read"* this prayer, letting the Holy Spirit work on you and until your prayer completes.

Every time we pray, the whole heavenly and earthly realm, Father, Son and Holy Spirit are all listening. Some of you may have a good start, but soon you may find that your environment and things seemingly become worse, these situations mostly come from the enemies' resistance because your prayers are effective and is starting to work. Do continue to pray, do not get discouraged, focus on the Lord's goodness, and continue to offer the sacrifices of praise, give thanks to Him, for He is faithful. (Read Daniel 10, see how the Lord sends Gabriel the first day when he starts to pray and seek the Lord, which caused a war in the Heavenlies. He prayed continuously for 21 days.) We encourage you to continue your prayer until you get the break through.

The purpose of this prayer book is to provide a guidance or reference for brothers and sisters in the body of Christ who need help. Please follow the Holy Spirit who is our helper, to add or change the way you pray.

3

We suggest you to use cleansing prayer to cut ungodly spirit, soul, and body links after you minister to people or intercede for them. If you still feel not totally cleansed yet, you can either pray in the spirit or continue use *"Declaration of Confidence in God's Protection (Nighttime proclamation for protection)"*, *"Proclaim of the Victory in Jesus Christ"*, to continue be set free. Remember to rest in the Lord and renew your strength. (Isaiah 30:15)

The Index contains some prayers for Deliverance ministry. We include these for people who need help. These prayers have been accumulated through our years of experience in ministering to Chinese and East Asian Christians. Many prayers are seemingly long but are for the purpose of removing all the enemy's rights deeply rooted in people's life. We do not encourage you to do self-deliverance, especially those who are used to be deeply involved in idolatry and occultism. We suggest you seek for brother/sisters to support you. Ideally have someone who has experiences of spiritual warfare. If you can find someone who has gift of discerning spirit would be best.

[Forward]

This translation took us 4 years to complete. When I first started, I did not realize the immense difficulties in translating from Chinese to English which is quite different from translating from English to Chinese. While I was working on the translation, I found that many of the areas in the Chinese culture is really difficult to find suitable English to describe it, especially the Chinese belief system, our idioms or old fashion way. Thank God, with His help and thanks to the internet, I was able to finish the first stage of translation.

When we need someone to edit my English, (frankly it's still pretty Chinese way of speaking English). I can't find suitable person to do so, everyone found it difficult. Of course I was too ignorant about the spiritual warfare we were facing. Finally, after seeking the Lord and prayer, we have our son Matthew to help with Christine's assistant, took another year to finish the initial editing process. When we need final editing, we realized that the only most suitable person is Tony, who can understand both the English reader and also the differences between Chinese culture and God's system, so that every prayer can be kept with the original meaning to help everyone who uses it. While we were nearly finished we found ourselves in spiritual warfare, Tony was being attacked severely and took much longer time to complete it.

Thanks to Matthew, Christine, and Tony, we have finished the task, so that those who are really in need can use this prayer book to help them to be set free and receive the abundant blessings that God has promised every believer, especially those English speaking Christian with East Asian background.

We also thank sister Elisha Y. H. Lee who first obeyed the Lord, putting our prayer together with other prayers to form the first prayer book and later also spent a lot of time to rewrite some of the prayers and added new prayer to finally form the whole book. Chinese version already has been published since 2009. More and more people learned to use it and helped them to change their life, for the better.

[Lordship Prayer]

Lord Jesus, I confess that I have sinned and I acknowledge my need of You. I thank You for dying on the cross for me and I accept You as my Savior. I invite You now to be Lord of every area and every moment of my life from the time I was conceived until now and forever.

Lord of my spirit, my spiritual senses, Lord of my conscience, intuition, and my relationship with You; Lord of my spiritual awareness and worship. Lord of my soul and the health of my soul, my mind, attitudes, beliefs, imagination, my thinking patterns, memories, judgments, my conclusions, my dreams and all the information I receive, and Lord of all my thoughts; Lord of my emotions, my expression of my feelings and all my reactions; Lord of my will and all my decisions; Lord of my defense mechanism, coping mechanisms and my behavior cycles.

Lord of my body, and Lord of my body's various organs and each gene, cells, and tissues, including the **Nervous system** 【brain (the brain, midbrain, cerebellum, medulla, basal ganglia) 】, spinal, sympathetic, para-sympathetic, nerve, sural nerve, touch and temperature, pain, proprioception, vision, hearing and balance, smell, taste, the brain electrical activity, posture

Motion Control, **Muscle system** 【skeletal muscle system, myocardium, smooth muscle】, **Endocrin system** 【metabolism, thyroid, parathyroid, pancreas carbohydrate metabolism, adrenal medulla and the cortex, hypothalamus, pituitary gland, gonads, pineal and other endocrine organs】 ; **Digestive system** 【mouth, teeth, tongue, esophagus, stomach, small intestine , colon, liver, gall bladder, spleen, pancreas, rectum, anus】 ; **Blood circulatory system** 【blood, lymph nodes, heart, valves, electrical activity of the heart, arteries, veins, micro vessels, blood pressure regulation, cerebral circulation, coronary circulation, splanchnic circulation】, skin cycle (pregnancy: placental and fetal blood circulation); **Respiratory system** 【nasal cavity, trachea , bronchus, lung, diaphragm, respiratory regulation】 ; **Urinary system** 【kidney, ureter, bladder, urethra and urine excretion】 ; **Reproductive system** 【Female: uterus, cervix, ovaries, fallopian tubes, vagina, the egg, the menstrual cycle, breast, breast gland male: My testicles, epididymis, vas deferens, spermatic vein, spermatic artery, seminal vesicle, prostrate, sperm)】 **The skeletal system** 【skull, spine, sternum and ribs, shoulder strap, hip, upper and lower limbs, joints, cartilage, bone, bone marrow, periosteum】, skin, nails, pores, sweat glands, perspiration and **Body temperature regulation system**, Lord of my **Immune system.**

My physical health, my symptom (fill in with symptoms you have at the moment while you are praying), my exercise, my nutrition, my rest, my appearance, my weight and all my behavior; Lord of my eyes, my eye sight, my visual system and what I look upon; Lord of my ears, hearing, auditory system, as well as all the voices and everything that I listen to; Lord of my mouth, my tongue, vocal cords, vocal organ, and what I speak; Lord of my hands and all that I do; and Lord of my feet and everywhere that I go; Lord of my sexuality and its expression; Lord of my time, my work, my ministry, my pleasure, my home, my family, my possessions, my perceived needs, my finances, my plans, my ambitions, my future and all my relationships. Thank you, Jesus, that Your blood was shed that I might be set free. Amen.

[Prayer to Put on God's Full Armor]

Lord Jesus, I dedicate to Thee my mind, and put on a helmet of salvation from You. From now on, I want to meditate Thee and Thy word; and any thoughts that is true, honest, just, pure, lovely, virtue and with good report. Lord, please help me not to allow any dirty thoughts of injustice stay in my mind.

Lord Jesus, I dedicate my eyes to Thee. From now on, I want to always focus on Thee alone, and behold your glory and holiness; Lord, please help me to watch whatever is pure, lovely, with good reputation, and virtuous on the nature of matter or material. Whatever that displeases You Lord, no matter what things, books, newspapers, television, movies, the Internet, or DVD I will not watch.

Lord Jesus, I dedicate my ear to Thee. From now on, I only listen to Thy voice and teachings, and those words are in line with Truth and words of exhortation, comfort and words of encouragement to my soul. Lord, please help me to eliminate any gossip or the threat of all, negative, complaining, criticism, argument, complaints, curses, bitterness, wrath, filthy, cheating, manipulation, domination, confused, and lying words in my environment. Help me not to listen, and if not avoidable they will not influence me; I also chose to forgive, bless and love every one whoever had spoken

10

these words to me.

Lord Jesus, I dedicate my lips to Thee, I would like to speak words that create comfort, encouragement, blessings to others. Any real, respectable, and justice, what virtue, what is praiseworthy; I will glorify Thee with my lips. Lord, help me not to speak any words of gossip or threat; any negative, complaining, criticism, argument, convictions, complaints, and cursed, bitterness, wrath, nasty, bullying, deception, manipulation, domination, confused, or lying.

Lord Jesus, I dedicate my will to Thee, I will put on the breast plate of Righteousness, Thy Righteousness covers my chest; Lord, please help me to keep my heart clean, honest and with good integrity. And girdle my loin with the belt of Truth; grant me the Spirit of wisdom and revelation. Therefore the Truth will reveal and embedded in my heart, so I can meditate day and night. Fill me with Thy love so that I can love God with all my heart and love one another; enable me to make anything decisions not to my will but to Thy will. I chose to be humble, and to forgive, love and bless others. Because I am not omniscient, I might be weak and wrong; I need to give grace to others to have opportunities to repent and change.

Lord Jesus, I dedicate my hands to Thee. I will take up the sword of the Spirit which is the word of God.

11

When I declare the Word of God, the power of the Word will complete the work of God. Also I will take up the shield of faith to extinguish all the flaming arrows of the evil one, to extinguish all negative, doubt, unbelief, and dispute. From now on, I will only work for You. Lord please help me, lead me to listen and follow the guidance of Holy Spirit. Lean on, trust in, and be confident in the Lord with all my heart and mind and do not rely on my own insight or understanding. In all my ways know, recognize, and acknowledge Him and He will direct and make straight and plain my paths. Help me that I will not touch anything that is not pleasing in Your sight, Lord!

Lord Jesus, I dedicate my feet to Thee, I put on the gospel of peace as a preparatory walking shoes; from now on, I will walk on the path that the Lord has called me to be my destiny. Lord, please help me, not to go to any place that is unpleasing to You. Anywhere that You did not command me to go, I will not go. In The Holy Name of Jesus Christ I pray. Amen. (Ephesians 6:10-18; Philippians 8.)

[Put On Full Armors of God (short)]

Good Morning! Holy Spirit! Good Morning! Lord Jesus! Good Morning! Abba Father!

In the name of Jesus Christ, I plead the Blood of Jesus Christ of Nazareth on myself, my family (name every family member in your home), my house, my work (ministry), work of my spouse, my finance, friends, pets, vehicles, health, church, pastors, bishop, cell group leader....etc. (name every one or everything that needs God's protection)

Dear heavenly Father, I offer my body as a living sacrifice to you, according to the Scripture, as this is holy and pleasing to you (Rom. 12:1). Father, I therefore put on the full armor of God, so that when the day of evil comes, I may be able to stand my ground, and after I have done everything, to stand. Stand firm then, with the belt of truth buckled around my waist, with the breastplate of righteousness in place, and with my feet fitted with the readiness that comes from the gospel of peace. In addition to all this, I will take up the shield of faith, with which I can extinguish all the flaming arrows of the evil one. I will take the helmet of salvation and the sword of the Spirit, which is the word of God. And pray in the Spirit on all occasions with all kinds of prayers and requests. With this in mind, I will be alert and always keep on praying for all the saints. Praying also for myself, that whenever I open my mouth, words may be given me so that I will fearlessly make known the mystery of the gospel (Eph. 6:14-19). According to the Scripture, The glory of the Lord will be my rear guard. (Isa. 58:8)

Father, I thank You and give all my praises to You for the full armor that You provided for me today. I declare in the name of Jesus Christ of Nazareth, that I am covered by the power of the blood that Jesus had shed for me. I build my life, my family, my marriage, my home on the foundation of the rock...Father, Son and Holy Spirit. Gates of Hades will not overcome it. The Lord is my shepherd, I shall not want (Psalm 23:1). My God will supply all my needs according to His glorious riches in Christ Jesus (Phil. 4:19). And I know I can do all things through Him who gives me strength. (Phil. 4:13). For though I walk in the flesh, I do not war according to the flesh, for the weapons of my warfare are not of the flesh, but divinely powerful for the destruction of fortresses. I am destroying speculations and every lofty thing that arises up against the knowledge of God, and I am taking every thought captive to the obedience of Christ. (II Cor. 10:3-5). I cast all my anxiety on You because You care for me. I give You all my praises, for you have given me the heavenly health, You have forgiven all my sins and iniquities, healed all my diseases (Psalm 103:3), and the punishment that brought us peace was upon You, and by Your wounds I am healed. (Isa. 53:5). I thank You and praise You that I may prosper in all things and be in health, just as my soul prospers (3 John 1:2), And I know that the peace of God, which transcends all understanding, will guard my heart and my minds in Christ Jesus (Phil. 4:7).

The joy of the Lord is my strength (Neh.8:10). O Lord, let your ear be attentive to the prayer of this your servant and to the prayer of your servants who delight in revering your name. Give your servant success today by granting him favor in the presence of this man." (Neh. 1:11)

Father, arise in me and manifest Your greatness, because I belong to you. In the name of Jesus Christ the Nazareth. Amen.

[Daily Prayer]

Dear Heavenly Father, I praise and honor Thee as my Savior and Lord of my life, You reign above all creation. I thank You for You are always with me, and never abandoned me. Only You are almighty God and omniscient, You show Your mercy and kindness and faithfulness in all You do. I love You. I thank You for joining me with Jesus Christ, and live in Him. I choose not to love the world and things of the world, and allow You to crucify all my flesh and evil desires.

I give you all my thanksgivings for my life in Christ. Please fill me with the Holy Spirit, empower me to say no to sin, say yes to Your will. I decree to depend on You and put all my trust in You. I am determined to reject Satan and all the lies that comes from him. By my will, I choose to believe the truth in the Scripture, regardless of my feeling. I reject all helplessness and hopelessness, because You are the source of all hope. There is nothing too difficult for you, therefore I trust that when I decide to do things according to Your Word, You will supply all my needs. Thank You, I believe that by the strength that Jesus Christ gives me, I can live a life that is satisfied, abundant and responsible.

Now I am determined to fight against Satan and all evil forces, I command all evil spirits to leave me. I choose to put on the full armor that You have given to me through my Lord Jesus Christ, so that I can resist all evil tactics of devil. I offer my body as living sacrifice to You, that is holy and pleasing to You. I choose to renew my mind with Your word, so that I can know what is Your good, pleasing and perfect will. In Jesus' name I pray. Amen.

[Fire Wall Protection Prayer]

Lord Jesus, I plead your blood over my whole family including _____ (list names of your house hold). Please place the power of cross in between each member of my family and also between us whomever we encounter today. Please stop the ungodly flow of powers of darkness to us. Protect us from all evil attacks from the enemy, including loss of property and finances, sickness, illnesses, diseases, pain, infections, defilements, inflammation, plagues, infectious diseases, allergy, viruses, hurt, disasters, trauma, crush, vilifications, panic, snatch, bully, oppression, stealing, killing, destruction, confusion, deception, toil, self-pity, anxiety, depression, worry, discourage, frustration, disappointment, withdraw, defeat, compromise, disturbance, chaos, accusation, evil or any accidents.

Please keep out any evil thoughts in our hearts, including homicide, adultery, hatred, thievery, illicit sexual relations, perversions, false testimonies, blasphemies (Matt. 15:19), coveting, dangerous and destructive wicked-ness, deceit; unrestrained (indecent) conduct; an evil eye (envy), slander (evil speaking, malicious misrepresentation, abusiveness), pride, foolishness (folly, lack of sense, recklessness, thoughtlessness) (Mark 7:22), judgments, control, selfishness.

Help us to have a heart that fears the Lord, obey His

commands, imitate His will, virtue, faith, generosity, tolerance, love, patience, submitting to one another in the fear of God (Eph. 5:21)

Keep us from all danger of this end time, shun away from evil, those who overly love themselves, lovers of money, boasters, those who are prideful, blasphemers, disobedient to parents, unthankful, unholy, [3]unloving, unforgiving, slanderers, without self-control, brutal, despisers of good, [4]traitors, headstrong, haughty, lovers of pleasure rather than lovers of God, having a form of godliness but denying its power.

If we are under any kinds of evil attacks from the power of darkness, any forms of witchcraft, sorceries, curses, spells, evil spirits, in Jesus' name I cancel the assignments of all these evil powers, and declare them null and void, and proclaim the blood of Jesus the Nazareth to repel all the curses, witchcrafts and sorceries, spells and attacks. I proclaim and plead the blood, the power of the cross of Jesus Christ to be placed between my family ancestral lines and my family members, including my spouse's family lines. Jesus' blood covers, cleanses us and breaks all these curses and any other evil effects from inherited sin and iniquities. The blood of Christ also removes any rights of the enemy due to ancestral sin and iniquities and turns every curse into double portion blessings.

19

If there are any evil spirit and/or human spirit which are sent to attack us, in the name of Jesus the Nazareth I cancel all your assignments, command you to stay down and be quiet. I bless every human spirit to know the Father Almighty God, the creator of the universe, and commit you into the hands of our Lord Jesus Christ. In Jesus' name I bind all the evil spirits and command you to go where Jesus sends you, never to return or hurt any other human being.

Lord Jesus! send your warrior angels to surround us, and cover my whole family _____(name family members) and over the location, time, space and materials we are in with Your blood, so that the enemy cannot come near us, nor attack us in any way. Father God, thank you for your promise, grace, mercy and protection for my family. Thank You, Father, for protecting our coming in and going out. We are blessed and favored in and out. We are blessed and favored in the city and in the field. We are blessed and favored with strength in our spirit, soul and body, and shall prosper in all things. In Jesus' name. Amen.

[Declaration of the Power of the Blood]

Note: Insert your name or person's name in all the blanks spots.

In Jesus' Name I declare that

The Blood of Jesus

1. Cleanse all the sins of _____. (1 Jn. 1:7)

2. Paid all the price for _____, redeemed_____.(I Cor. 6:20)

3. Make _____ Holy, faultless and irreproachable in His [the Father's] presence. (Col. 1:22)

4. All the sins of _____ were forgiven, and therefore no more condemnation. (Rom 8:1)

5. Made _____ alive, when _____were dead (slain) by _____'s trespasses and sins. (Eph. 2:1)

6. Delivered _____ From law of sin and death. (Rom. 8:2)

7. Put an end to the handwriting of the law which was against _____, and nailed it to his cross; (Col. 2:14)

8.   Restored _____ 's spirit and life. (Psalm 23, 1Pet 1:3)

9.   Made _____ born again and receive eternal life. (Jh. 3:16)

10.   Gives _____ right to be the child of God, to be adopted as His son. (Jn. 1:12)

11.   Reconciled _____ with Father God, to come near Him. (Col.1:22)

12.   Made _____ to enter into the Holy of Holies.

13.   Made _____ to receive the Spirit of His Son, to call Him Abba Father. (Gal.4:6)

14.   Make _____ to receive mercy and grace as help in times of need from Father God. (Heb. 4:16)

15.   Made _____ a new creation

16.   Made _____ a member of God's household. (Eph.2:19)

17.   Made _____ a royal priesthood. (1 Pet. 2:9)

18.   Made _____ a people of Holy nation. (1 Pet. 2:9)

19. _____ received abundant and resurrected life. (John. 10:10)

20. Made ____ to receive the abundant inheritance of Kingdom of God. (Col. 2:9,10, Eph. 3:6)

21. Made _____ enter into blessings and redeemed _____ from curses. (Gal. 3:13,14)

22. Made _____ seated with him in the heavenly realms in Christ Jesus. (Eph. 2:6)

23. Caused _____ to receive peace and be healed. (Isa. 53:5)

24. Redeemed _____ from poor and to have wealth. (2 Cor. 8:9)

25. Caused _____ renounce falsity and receive truth.

26. Caused _____ come out of darkness and enter into His light. (1 Pet. 2:9)

27. Caused _____ to receive every spiritual blessing of heavenly realms and inherited the inheritance of Abraham. (Eph. 1:3, Gal. 3: 7-9,29)

28. _____ have authority over the devil. (Mat.

23

10:1, Lk. 9:1)

29. _____ have authority to cast out demons. (Mat. 10:1, Lk. 9:1)

30. _____ have dominion ship over the earth, to reign with Christ Jesus on earth. (Rev. 5:10)

31. _____ has authority to heal the sick. (Mat. 10:1, Lk. 9:1)

32. Caused _____ has authority to resurrect the dead.

33. Caused _____ has authority to make lepers clean.

34. Caused _____ has authority to preach the gospel of Kingdom of God. (Mat. 10:8)

[Cleansing Prayer After Daily Activities]

Thank You, Jesus, for dying that I might be forgiven. By an act of my will I now choose to forgive those who have hurt or defiled me _____(name out loud the people that need to be forgiven). I release each and every one of these people into the freedom of my forgiveness. I bless them to have every blessing that God has promised.

In the name of the Father, the Son and the Holy Spirit, I break all ungodly spirit, soul and body links that have been established between me and _____(speak out the name of the individual involved). I ask You, Lord, to return to me every part of myself which has been wrongfully tied in bondage to (again name the person). I ask that You remove from me all ungodly influences that has come from (name the person again). I ask you, Father, to place the cross of Jesus and His shed blood between us and stop all ungodly flow between us. In Jesus' name.

I now speak directly to every evil spirit that has taken advantage of this ungodly linking. In the name of Jesus, I bind you and rebuke you and command you to leave me now, go where Jesus takes you, never to return, hurt or harm any other person. I command you to go quietly, causing no manifestation; you have no more rights here. In Jesus' name.

Any human spirit, I commit you, dead to dead, living to living, to go where Jesus destine you to go. Go in peace. In Jesus' name. Amen.

Lord, Jesus, I now cast all my burdens to You. Thank you, that You are the Lord who carries all our burdens daily, and You have promised us that Your burden is light and Your yolk is easy.

Once again, Lord, I ask for the cleansing power of Your shed blood to cleanse me from all defilement that has been affected me/us during ministry. Thank You for your protection and promises. In Jesus' name. Amen

[Declaration of Confidence in God'Protection]

(Nighttime Proclamation for Protection)

Our Father in heaven, thank You that You are our protector, our help comes from You, who made heaven and earth. The battle belongs to You, _____(name names of family members and people you cover) are your children, You will guard our going out and our coming in from this time forth and forever. Thank You Father for keeping us until now, and You will continue to guard us until our old age and even to our graying years You will carry us (Isaiah 46:3-4). We are Your children and You called us by name, You made us righteous when we believed that Jesus Christ as Your only begotten son to be our savior, that we would be holy and blameless before You in love.

Now I decree according to Your promise, "No weapon that is formed against us shall prosper and every tongue which rises against us in judgment we do condemn. This is our heritage as servants of the Lord and our righteousness is of You. O Lord of Hosts." (Isaiah 54:17) If there are those who have been speaking or praying against us, criticizing and judging us, seeking harm or evil by performing rituals, witchcraft, praying to false god/s, or cursing toward us or who have rejected us, we forgive them and release them, having forgiven them, we bless them in the name of the Lord (Matt. 5:43, Rom.

27

12:14). In Jesus' name, I declare all curses, evil and negative words and witchcraft rituals as null and void, have no ill effect to us.

Now we declare, O Lord Jesus, that You and You alone are our Lord and Savior, and besides You there is no other—a just God and a Savior, the Father, the Son and the Spirit—and we worship You!

We submit ourselves afresh to You tonight in unreserved obedience. Having submitted to You, Lord, we do as Your Word directs. We resist the devil: all his pressures, his attacks, his deceptions, every instrument or agent he would seek to use against us. We do not submit! We resist him, drive him from us and exclude him from us in the Name of Jesus. Specifically, we reject and repel: infirmity, pain, Infection, inflammation, malignancies, allergies, viruses, accidents, trauma, crush, attack, disaster, bully, oppression, depression, distress, horror, poverty, robbery, stealing, killing, destruction, disturbance, confusion, deception, lie, accusation, fighting, despising, jealousy, envy, leisure, self-satisfying, distrust, guessing, defilement, lust, negotiating, compromising, laborious, fear, withdraw, worry, anxiety, annoying, self-pity, despair, frustration, impatient, chaos, disappointment, failure, comparison, competition, exhaustion and every form of witchcraft. In Jesus' name, I command you to leave me, never to return, never to hurt anybody. Any human spirit, that

28

sent to attack and influence us, I bless you and commit you dead to dead, *living to living, to the hands of Jesus Christ, you can go in peace. Father God, I ask that You send warrior angels to help us to win this victory, fulfill all the works.

Finally, Lord, we thank You that through the sacrifices of Jesus on the Cross, we have passed out from under the curse and enter into all blessings of heavenly places and earthly realm, as we reconcile with You and call You Abba Father. Thank You that You prepared a table before me in the presence of my enemies; You have anointed my head with oil; My cup overflows (Psalm 23:5). I receive my abundant blessings: exaltation, health, abundance, prosperity, victory, God's favor (Gal. 3:13-14, Gen. 24:1). In Jesus' Name. Amen.

Modified from prayers of Derek Prince

[Prayer Before Sleep]

Dear Heavenly Father! I come before you to cast all my burdens to You, please search my mind, my words, my deeds, to see if I have done evil in Your sight. Please convict me, so that I can confess and repent before You. I ask that You cleanse me with the blood of Jesus again, forgive me for any secret sin, and any sin of my deeds, words, attitudes, and thoughts. *[Pray in Spirit, use tongues..... pray for a while, and then wait quietly for a while, if Lord reveal anything or issue or people, and then you should exam and confess, repent or forgive, let the Holy Spirit lead you. If you have any anxiety, or worry or negative emotions, cast your burden unto Him, talk to Him as if He is your best friend and express your heart to Him]*

Thank You Father, for forgiving me all my sins, please help me to know You more, love You deeper, renew me again, give me a clean spirit and a right heart, so that I will hate sin, shun evil and have reverential fear of You. Once again, I offer myself unto You, my Lord Jesus Christ, my spirit, soul and body, all of me, all to You. Please come and fill me and sit on the throne of my life, be the Lord of every area, every moment of my life, be the Lord of my sleep, my environment. I will rest in Your arms in peace, still I will praise You when I wake up.

Father God, You are the God of peace. Please sanctify me through and through [separate me from profane things, make me pure and wholly consecrated to God]; and make it so my spirit, soul and body be preserved, sound and complete [and found] blameless at the coming of our Lord Jesus Christ (the Messiah). Protect my spirit, soul and body in my sleep, so that I can sleep tight, peaceful and have restful slumber, no dreams form evil or dreams of temptation. My spirit guard and alert me in my dream, even in my sleep, my spirit will be built, edified, healed, and renewed, my spirit will commune with triune God even in my sleep. The Lord sustains me, whether I am asleep or awake and I give thanks to Him.

Lift up the light of Your countenance upon us, O Lord. You have put more joy and rejoicing in my heart than [they know] when their wheat and new wine have yielded abundantly. In peace I will both lie down and sleep, for You, Lord, alone make me dwell in safety and gain confidence and trust in this land, world and earth. The Lord gives [blessings] to His beloved in sleep (Psalm 127:2), I am His beloved, I shall receive blessings in my sleep. In Jesus' name I pray. Amen.

[Prayer to Cleanse the House]

Father God, I come before you in the name of Jesus and the power of the Holy Spirit, I acknowledge You. You are the Lord of my life, and the Lord of this place, please reveal to me any events and sins that has happened, but not been confessed and repented in this place. As the owner of this place, I ask You to forgive all the sins that have been done against You on this land and in this house. I also choose to forgive everyone who has sinned against You and brought evil influences to us on this land and in this house. I release them into the freedom of my forgiveness and bless them. Lord I also ask You to forgive all our secret faults and sins. I plead the Blood of Jesus to break all the bondages on this house (room/land) from the demonic powers. Lord Jesus! By the power of Your cross, and the Truth of Your Words, I pray Your Spirit to come and cleanse my home of all evil. In the holy name of Jesus we break all curses and evil declaration over this house (room/ land), declaring they are null and void, and sanctify this house and this land, giving its ownership to our Lord Jesus Christ and Father God.

I now speak directly to every evil spirit that has taken advantage of these sins. In the name of Jesus, I bind you and rebuke you and command you to leave this house (room/land) now, go where Jesus takes you, never to return, hurt or harm any other person. I command you to go quietly, you have no more rights here. In Jesus' name.

Any human spirit, I commit you into the hand of Lord Jesus'. I also commit the dead to the dead, the living to the living. Go where Jesus has destined for you to go. Go in peace. Father God, please send Your warrior angels to help us to fight this battle and complete all this work. In Jesus' name. Amen.

Lord Jesus, please fill this place with your holy presence. Reign and use this place according to Your Will. We ask that You will act according to Your Word. Station Holy angels to surround the boundary of this property, covering and protecting us from evil. (John 17:15;2 Thessalonians 3:3) Holy Spirit, we welcome You. Please come and fill this house, fill the byways and air ways of this house and land and make this place your sanctuary. I declare the evil ones have no right to remain here. I pray in the name of Jesus, whose name is above all name, the King of kings, and the Lord of lords. Amen.

[Daily Prayer for House Cleaning]

(If your house still contains items from idol worship that come from other family members, please strengthen the daily prayer over your house, and apply the blood of the Lord Jesus to cover yourself and other Christians at home and in every area and every corner within the house.)

Dear Abba Father, please forgive our trespasses today and all of the secret faults and sins, especially our incomplete word. I ask for the Blood of the Lord Jesus to cleanse us and our house. Cleanse every room and every corner, and sanctify this house for you. In Jesus' name I break and cancel all ungodly words of our mouths, please continue to help us and make the words from our mouth and thoughts in our minds to be pleasing in Your sight. Abba Father, I/We ask you to send your army of holy angels to be stationed around this house and to bind all of the darkness and evil spirits, that they be taken take to where Jesus wants them to go, and never to come back, nor hurt anyone else. Any human spirit that may have been sent by an evil power, I commit you into the hands of Jesus Christ, you may go, dead to dead, living to living, and to where Jesus sends you to go, go in peace. In the holy name of the Lord Jesus Christ. Amen.

[Cleansing Prayer for Rented Place and Room]

Dear Father God, I praise you, because the whole earth belongs to the Lord, I declare this place Yours. I come before you in the name of Jesus and in the power of the Holy Spirit. As Your child I declare the right as the inhabitant of this place, and ask You to forgive any sin and transgressions that has been committed in this room/place, or any other actions against You. I also choose to forgive everyone who has impacted my life, who has sinned against God, and release them into the freedom of my forgiveness, and bless them. I also ask you to forgive us of any unrevealed sin and trespasses.

I plead the blood of Christ, to cover and cleanse of all of the blasphemous actions that had been done in this room, and in the name of Jesus Christ I break all of the curses and oaths in this room, and declare they are null and void, and cannot affect me. Any evil spirits that have been disturbing this place, and this room, I now bind you in the name of Jesus, I break your power and command you to leave this place, go where Jesus takes you, never to return, and do not disturb or harm anyone. Any human spirit, I commit you, dead to dead, living to living, to go where Jesus destine you to go. Go in peace. In Jesus' name. Amen. Abba Father, please send your holy warrior angels to help us fight, and completed all these works. In the name of Jesus. Amen.

Lord Jesus, please fill this place with your holy presence, and reign in this place during the time when I live here. Father God please send your guardian angels to station here and protect Your children from all the doings of the evil one, and give peace to my spirit, soul and body. In the name of Jesus. Amen.

[Proclaim of Victory in Jesus Christ]

(We suggest those who are in spiritual warfare, pray the "Lordship prayer", "Put on full armor prayer", "Prayer for fire wall protection" to pray for protection first. If you know your spouse or parents are still involve in idol worship or cult activity, please use "Cleansing prayer" first, so that enemy can't use these ungodly soul ties to attack you. May you rise and shine for the Lord, and you are light and salt)

Father, Son and Holy Spirit, triune almighty God! Only You are the true God, our only King, the only Lord. You are the ruler of all things, the whole universe belongs to You, all above, under the sea, all the earth, and in the air, all which are Yours. You are omnipotent, omniscient, omnipresence God! All things are created by You, nothing is not created by You. Your word is sent out, and it is done. You sent Your decree and it is complete. You support all things by Your word of power. Oh Lord! You are the creator of the universe! THE HEAVENS declare the glory of God and the firmament shows and proclaims Your handiwork, day after day pours forth speech, and night after night shows forth knowledge. Yet Your voice [in evidence] goes out through all the earth, Your sayings to the end of the world. The whole universe bow down before You and worship You.

Father God! We plead the blood of Jesus Christ over us,

also we ask for the power of cross to be put in between us and all powers of darkness, to form a protective shield. I surrender myself all to You, I reject and renounce all the works of Satan in my life. I only commune with the living God, and I eagerly desire to be filled with the full (deep and clear) knowledge of the Father's will in all spiritual wisdom [in comprehensive insight into the ways and purposes of God] and in understanding and discernment of spiritual things. I reject and rebuke all the distractions of Satan's work in my prayer and my life. In the name of Jesus, I bind all the spirits of confusion, delusion, bewilderment, heaviness, faintness, and oppression. Satan, I command you and all your agents and cohorts to leave me. Father God, please sent Your warrior angels to surround us, protect us and fulfill all the works of our prayers.

Father God! All honor, glory, blessings, and praises I give to You! You are the Lord of my life and You are my all in all. Lord Jesus! I surrender all to You, I belong to You and You alone. I ask that the Holy Spirit come fill me, permeate me, guide me and lead me to the path that the Lord has chosen for me; teach me and help me pray. Thank You Father for loving me and choosing me from the beginning, You sent Your only begotten Son to this world to die for me, redeeming all my sin. Thank You Lord Jesus that You died for me and become my holy scapegoat, I can be righteous when I believed in You. I deeply believe,

God has forgiven all my sins, I can enter into the Kingdom of Son, I am holy and blameless, and above reproach in Father's sight.

Search me, O God, and know my heart; Try me, and know my anxieties; and see if there is any wicked way in me, reveal to me any weaknesses and any foot holds that enemy still have in my life; convict me of anything in my life that is not pleasing in Your sight. Help me, give me strength and understanding, so that I can confess and repent and forgive so I can close all these foot holds. I will no longer accept enemy's attacks and accusations, make me hide under Your wings, dwell in Your secret place. By the power You strengthened me with, I can live a life to glorify Your name.

✝ In Jesus' name, I cancel all the assignments of all principalities, powers, the rulers of the darkness of this age, and spiritual hosts of wickedness in the heavenly places, I command you to cease all your activities. Jesus Christ had crushed the headship of Satan, destroyed all rulers and principalities, and those who had power over death, Jesus declared His victory openly. All authority of heaven and earth belongs to Jesus Christ, every knee shall bow, and every tongue confess that Jesus Christ is Lord.

✝ In Jesus' name, I renounce and reject all strong holds of temptation, hint, accusation, negative emotion, zealous, hindrances, lying, deception, and distortion of truth and secular views that come from Satan. I chose only to believe in God's word of Truth.

✠ In Jesus' name I declare, I will strip off my old nature, and put on the new nature (the regenerate self) created in God's image, enter into the victory of finished work that Jesus had completed on the cross, that all my sins has been cleansed, and live a life that overcome all sins.

✠ In Jesus' name, I proclaim that by the power of the Holy Spirit, I strip off all the old nature of selfishness, fear, weaknesses, guile, desires of flesh, and I put on the new nature of Love, kindness, strength, boldness, righteousness and holiness enter into the resurrection and victorious glory of the Son.

Dear Holy Spirit! I welcome you, come and fill me, saturate me, permeate me, so that I can be filled by You all the time, full of Your presence, to bear fruits of love, joy (gladness), peace, patience (an even temper, forbearance), kindness, goodness (benevolence), faithfulness, gentleness (meekness, humility), and self-control (self-restraint, continence). Help me to discern all the tactics of Satan, destroy all the strong holds that Satan has in my mind.

Precious Holy Spirit! Please come and help me, so that

I can surrender all to You. I will not lean on my own insight or understanding, and not be wise in my own eyes. I will hate sin and love sinners, and in all the ways acknowledge You. Listen to Your voice, and obey Your guidance, and not quench any sanctions You give to me.

Dear heavenly Father, I praise You and thank You for the life you gave to me, the good plan you have for me, all the heavenly spiritual blessings, and blessings of offspring of Abraham, the inheritance that You have measured for me, all the promises You prom-ised me, You watch over me and never slumber, You watch over me all my life forever and ever. I offer my spirit, soul and body all to You, I will rejoice because of Your goodness and loving kindness, You gave me a heart of Christ, Father's thoughts is my thoughts, allowing You to be the Lord and head in my life. I pray and give thanks in the name of Jesus. Amen.

[Declare God's Protection (during attacks)]

(When you are attacked, please open your mouth to sing praises to God, if you are too weak to sing, you can use stereo, TV, or other radio equipment to play praise and worship songs and sing along with it. It's best to use songs that proclaim the blood of Christ, and salvation. Continue to declare and ask the Lord to draw the blood boundary in the spirit, ask for protection, and continue to worship until God's throne and His peace are established.)

In the Jesus' name, Father God please draw the boundary of Christ's blood around me to stop all attacks from powers of darkness. Bind all power of darkness and the evil spirits. Father God! You will guard the feet of Your saints, but the wicked shall be silent in darkness, (1 Samuel 2:9) I ask You Lord to send angels to fight for me, that I may complete all assignments and fulfill my destiny.

Lord, You are my rock, my fortress, my stronghold, my refuge, my pillar, I ask You to hide me under Your wings, the shelter of Your hiding place, You control what happens in my life, I'm led by You from the corner of the earth, You say to me I am Your servant, You've chosen me and do not forsake me, I'm not afraid, because You are with me. I'm not dismayed, because you are my God. You will strengthen me, help me, and lift me up with Your righteous right hand. All those who were incensed against me shall be ashamed and disgraced; they shall be as nothing, those who oppose me will be as nothing and perish. Though I search for my enemies, I will not find them. Those who wage war against me will be as nothing at all. For You, the LORD my God, will hold my right hand, saying to me, *"Fear not, I will help you. And your Redeemer, the Holy One of Israel. Behold, I will make you into a new threshing sledge with sharp teeth; you shall thresh the mountains and beat them small, and make the hills like chaff."* (Isaiah 41:9-16)

Thank you for sending your only begotten Son Jesus Christ to borne my grief, sins, and carry my sorrows, in the name of Jesus, I stand in the Truth of the Word of God: And declare the Son of God is manifested, that He might destroy the works of the devil. (1 John 3:8) To stop all actions by the power of darkness. Holy Spirit please reveal to me any sins that might have caused any foothold (then quiet down and pray either in your mind or tongues, pay attention to thoughts and memories that pass through your mind, pray until you feel peace)

Satan, here I denounce you and all of your doings in my life. Using my will and the power given to me by Jesus of Nazareth, I close these doors to you forever, I remove your right from taking away my joy and fruits of salvation. I command you in the name of Jesus, do not bother me on these issues. I have already renounced, repented these sins, and have been washed clean by the Blood of Jesus. Amen.

Any demonic spirit that is associated with the sins I have confessed above, in the name of Jesus, I command those power of darkness that have been ordered and sent to me, or surrounding me to leave right now, go where Jesus command you to go, and do not return. In the name of Jesus. Amen.

Father God, please send your angels to camp and surround to rescue me, I declare that all battles belong to the Lord. Father God, send Your angels to fight for me, that Your fire go before me to burns up my enemies, (Psalm 97:3; 50:3) Your lighting strikes the evil one. (Psalm 97:4) I believe when I depend on You, You will protect me. I believe the One within me is greater than he who is in the world.

Jesus Christ, I give you my spirit, my soul, and my body, I pray that you will protect, guard, and watch over me, and hide me under your wings; in the Shelter of the Rock, without your permission, no harm and disaster can fall upon me. Thank you for giving me the authority to overcome any attacks, and stump on all snakes and scorpions, the power of Hades cannot overcome me, in the name of Jesus I pray. Amen.

[Cry out for Holy Spirit]

Dear Holy Spirit, thank You for You are my Parakleotos, You are my teacher, comforter. You are the spirit of Truth, who leads me into truth, You are my helper, my seal of redemption, You are my guarantee of my inheritance. Most of all, You are the God who lives in me and the God who surrounds me, You are the Spirit of Son, lead me to cry for Abba Father! You are the one make me strong and courageous! You are the Spirit who caused Jesus to raise from the dead, You are Spirit of Christ, the Spirit of revelation and wisdom, the Spirit of knowledge, Spirit of understanding, Spirit of counsel and might, and the Spirit of fear of the Lord, and You are the Spirit that knows and searches all things. Holy Spirit, how I need You! Holy Spirit, come and fill me now, fill me thoroughly. I open myself up totally, please pour Your Spirit over me and let it flow in me, fill my dry and weary spirit, I hunger to be touched by You more, more possessed by You. I eagerly desire Your presence, please come and cleanse me, heal me, transform me, make my life to be cleansed, satisfied. I long for You like a deer pants for water. Please walk with me in every moment of my life.

Holy Spirit! Please fall upon me, fill me greatly, let the power of the most high over shadow me. Let the river of the Living water flow out of my belly, flow out from Your love, power, joy, peace, let my mouth speak of

Your word, goodness and kindness, let everyone to be blessed when they are in touch with me. Let all kinds of joy and peace fill my heart, so I may abound in hope by the power of the Holy Spirit (Rom. 15:13).

Oh, Spirit of Truth! I eagerly ask that You can help me, lead me, abide in me forever and dwell with me and in me. (John 14: 16-17). Holy Spirit, You are the spirit of wisdom and revelation and the spirit who searches all things, please make me able to receive the word of knowledge, word of wisdom. Fill me with divine goodness and kindness. Help me to overcome all evil trials and temptation, enlighten my eyes of understanding, so that I can really know Father God, not only by knowledge, but also by personal relationship with Him, that I may experience the depth, width, length and height of His love. Let me understand His will in my life, and also to understand the mystery of His will in Christ. Support my weaknesses, and intercede for me. (Rom 8:26), make me know You more and love You deeper.

Oh, Spirit of healing God, please pour out God's love into my heart. Comfort me, fill my heart and give me new hope (Rom 5:5). Heal all diseases in my spirit, soul and body. Renew me by Your Spirit to love God and man and to glorify Your name. Thank You for giving me gifts, for You are the Spirit who gives life (2 Cor. 3:6) All the fullness of the Godhead bodily dwells in

Christ, and I am complete in Him and through You Holy Spirit, the fullness of the Godhead bodily also dwells in me (Colossians 2:9). I will eagerly desire the gift of Holy Spirit, also love (1 Cor. 14:1). So that, I can glorify Father God.

Pour upon us Lord! O, Holy Spirit, who pour blessings unto us. Holy Spirit pour upon us from on high, and let the wilderness becomes a fruitful field, and the fruitful field is valued as a forest.(Isa.32:15)

Oh, Holy Spirit, You give us all good gifts from Father God. Please grant us God's promises that in the last day. You will pour out of Your Spirit on all mankind, our sons and our daughters shall prophesy and our young men shall see visions and our old men shall dream dreams and on Your menservants also and on Your maidservants in these days You will pour out of Your Spirit, and they shall prophesy. (Act 2:16-18). Oh, Holy Spirit! Please come and pour unto me, fill me up, so that I can speak in tongues, sing spiritual songs, pray in spirit. Please help me to give You more areas in my life. Let more of Your fruit grow in me, the fruit of love, joy, peace, patience, kindness, goodness, faithfulness, gentleness, self-control (Galatians 5:22-23). Give us the spirit of unity among everyone who was born of the Spirit, let us not quench the unction that You give us, let us who have ear to hear, and can see clearly, understand the Father's will, and follow

You closely. Let the Father's kingdom come, and His will to be done on earth as it is in heaven.

Fall upon us, Oh Holy spirit! We shall receive power from above and boldly preach the Kingdom, the way and the truth of God. We shall be witnesses to the Lord in Jerusalem, and in all Judea and Samaria, and to the ends of the earth. (Act 1:8, 4:31). Help us, by the strength and power you give us, to do all things, that I might be a minister of Jesus Christ to the Gentiles, ministering the gospel of God, that the offering of the Gentiles might be acceptable, sanctified by the Holy Spirit, and also be obedient people in God's kingdom. (Rom. 15:16-18)

Holy Spirit! I welcome you, please fill me, pour on me, renew me, and anoint me! Help me to be sanctified by you (1 Peter 1:2), so that I can live a life of a son/daughter of the living God. Let the glory of Father's grace to be praised. Amen.

[Prayer for the Restoration of Human Spirit]

Father God, in accordance with the richest treasury of Your glory and the work of the Holy Spirit who is living and working in me, fill me with Your mighty power and saturate me completely. Continually restore and renew me in my spirit, soul, and body to transform me into the likeness of Christ, and do not cease in maturing and growing me until I attain the stature of fullness of the Christ and the completeness found in Him.

Restore my crushed (crushed spirit) and bruised areas, back to the originally created structure and shape. Deliver me from parts in captivity and imprisonment (imprisoned spirit), set them free from all confinements and bondages. Heal my broken (broken spirit) and hurting areas. Transform my timid (timid spirit) parts to be bold and strong, and awake the ones that have slumbered (slumbered spirit). Cleanse my defiled (defiled spirit) areas, and guide my lonely (Orphaned spirit) parts to find their eternal home in Your arms. Feed the starved ones with in me (starved spirit) with your rich fattening nourishment, let the starved spirit be nurtured and satisfied in You. Turn my rebellious (spirit that turned away from God) parts toward you, and allow my wandering (unanchored spirit) ones to dwell and abide in You and be deeply rooted in Your love. Grant my worried, depressed, discouraged, and disappointed parts to find

49

peace, rest, hope, and joy. Strengthen and reinforce my inner man to be strong and powerful, and enable me to understand and experience together with the rest of your disciples the height, breadth, length, and depth of Your amazing and complete love.

Please align my spirit, soul, and body according to Your created order, that I may be wholly filled (through all my being) unto all the fullness of God, that I may have the richest measure of Your divine presence, and become a body wholly filled and flooded with God Yourself (Eph. 3). Restore me to the being You created. In the precious name of Jesus. Amen.

[Declaration for Whole Family]

In the name of the Lord Jesus Christ the Nazareth, I decree that things the Lord wants to complete in my family lines are higher than what I can ever think of, He will receive all the glory in my family.

I acknowledge that the Lord has a divine and wonderful plan and purpose for my family. I decree and call forth that the Lord's plan for _____(list the name of family members) to be complete at the earliest possible time. I call forth for every blessing and good gifts that the Lord prepared for them to fall upon them now! I declare that this is the year that the Lord has made to bless my family!

I declare that salvation of the Lord comes upon _____ (name everyone in family line that are not saved yet).

I command all the spirit of confusion and deception that blind fold them to leave now, and I ask for the Lord's mercy to open the eyes of their heart, they may see God's love for them. I declare that the devil has no power or influences over them. Thank you, Father that my family has received all the grace and mercy you have given to us.

Thank you, Father God for sending forth angels as ministering spirits to minister to those who shall be heirs of salvation (Hebrew 1:14). Please send your angels to minister to my family and bring the harvest of soul into my family line.

Thank You, Lord, I believe that the fatness of Holy Spirit will break the yoke of my family line, and all our heavy burdens will depart from our shoulders. (Isaiah 10:27). Thank You, Lord, that Your anointing removes all our heavy burdens and releases the garment of praise. Thank You Lord, Your anointing brings in your glorious beauty to replace the ashes in our life.

Thank You Lord, that Holy Spirit will reveal the Truth for my Family. The Truth is not a philosophy, but a person, He has a wonderful name, His name is above all names, His name is Jesus Christ; He is the Way, The Truth and The Life. In His great and mighty name, I declare, Jesus will manifest in every area of our life.

Lord, thank You that Your anointing will restore and renew the generational ruins of my family line. You are rebuilding all that the enemy have robbed from us, Your blessings endures forever. Your word will not go in vain, You always complete what You have willed for us.

For as many as are the promises of God, we all find their Yes [answer] in You [Jesus Christ]. For this reason we also utter the Amen (so be it) to God through You [in Your Person and by Your agency] to the glory of God. Amen.

[Prayers for the Blessing of Whole Family]

Dear Father God, thank You for sending Your beloved Son Jesus Christ to be sacrificed for all mankind. He paid the price for our sin, and bought me back. He opened this new and living pathway and led me back to Your home. Through Him You have given me the privilege to be Your child, a priest of Kingdom of God (II Peter 2:9). That I can enjoy the abundant blessings you have prepared for me, since the time You created heavens and earth. Thank You Father for you have given me every blessings in the heavenly places and all the abundant blessings as the heir of Abraham (Galatians 3:29). Thank you for every one of us that was saved because of Your free grace and through our faith, not of our own work. (Eph. 2:8-9) Thank You that by Your Grace I receive all the blessings and that I can come before You to know You, and My Lord Jesus Christ and Holy Spirit, the Triune God. I believe in Your word that my family and I have received Your grace.

Father, I pray that You will favor my family and I, You will favor my parents, and my children. my relatives, according to Your promises to help my whole family, open our eyes, that we may see; open our ears that we can hear Your word of love, mercy and grace. I also ask that the God of our Lord Jesus Christ, the Father of glory, that You may grant us a spirit of wisdom and revelation [of insight into mysteries and secrets] into the [deep and intimate] knowledge of You. By having the eyes of our heart flooded with light, so that we can know and understand the hope to which You have called us to, and know how rich is Your glorious inheritance in us the saints (His set-apart ones). Help us to have intimate relationships with You, Father God, so that we will understand Your decrees and have reverential fear of You, hate sin, turn away from evil, follow all Your laws, and precepts and command; and we will do justly, and to love kindness and mercy, and to humble ourselves and walk humbly with You, our God. (Micah 6:8) Help us to be humble and submissive so that we can receive all the blessings You have promised us. All the blessings in the heavenly realm and the blessings You have promised to the offspring of Abraham, let all the promises in Christ fulfill in every life of my family members that every family member of this house will sanctify ourselves and cast off all idols and worship You alone. Give us a heart of flesh to replace our heart of stone, give us a fresh spirit of Your Son, the spirit of Truth, and engrave the scripture on our hearts and spirit.

Lord, help us that we will be devoted in our behavior and keep on the watch with prayer, and guard our heart, and keep a grateful heart. Always count on Your grace, mercy and blessings as offerings of thanksgiving, to glorify Your name. Help us to teach Your ways to our children, please also bless our children that they can do so as well. (Duet. 4:9-10) Please grant our family members with a hungry heart for your righteousness and justice, deeply drawn by Your love, and the love to spread Your Word and Kingdom. Let us too, strongly desire a close, loving relationship and fellowship with The Father, Son and the Holy Spirit. We can also be sensitive to the unction and fellowship of the Holy Spirit, to have good discernment, and not quench the Spirit. Be Bold and not fear, having a good conscience, submitting to You with faith and perseverance.

Thank You Father, you have made our sins and iniquities go as far as east is from the west, by the redemption work Jesus has completed on the cross. Please help us to renounce all lies, and release the spirit of grace and supplication, so that we can come before You to seek Your face and Truth. You will convict us from all the traditions of man and philosophies, vain deceit and rudiments of this world, we can renounce them and choose to love Truth and reject all unrighteousness. Help us the whole family be totally set free from all the enemy's attack, deceptions, lies, confusion and oppression. Let Your redemptive work through Jesus become reality in every life of my family members. Help us to hold all our minds captive, let them all submit to Jesus Christ our Lord. Crush and break open all the enemy's strong hold in our lives and set us free from all the prisons.

Oh! Lord Jesus Christ, Please help us by setting us free from enemy's tactics especially in the areas of our emotion. Release Your healing power to remove all the evil root of enemy's bondage (wrath, rebellion, rejection, frustration, insecurity, disgust, comparison, competition, jealousy, shame, pride, stubbornness, self-righteousness, confusion, unbelief, doubt, nightmare, forgetfulness, lying, curse, deception, criticism, complain, blasphemy, bitterness, unforgiving, anxiety, worry, nervousness, fear, valuelessness, worthlessness, helplessness, pessimism, passiveness, fatalism, self-condemnation, perfectionism....) Set us free from all fear, set our mind to follow Your example: forgive ourselves and those who hurt us. Open our heart to receive Your mercy and grace, to desire Your presence, to be a witness for You to the ends of the earth. Thank You for accepting us just as we are. Thank You for never leaving us nor forsake us, please always grant us hope to trust You and all Your promises in the scripture.

Holy Spirit! Please help us to remove all the veils of our family, so that we have eyes to see, ears to hear, and make our hearts clear to follow You. Please release the spirit of revelation, let the Son of living God manifested in our lives, that He might destroy the works of the devil (I John 3:5-8). Help us to remove all the blindness, confusion and lies from enemy in our mind, help us to receive the wisdom from above in order to understand the Truth, and receive wisdom and spiritual discernment from God. For God, being full of mercy, through the great love which he has for us, even when we were dead through our sins, gave us life together with Christ (it is by grace you have salvation). (Eph. 2:4-5)

Oh! Father God! Please help everyone in my family to know we are the apple of Your eye, and we are the royal priest of your Kingdom and Your beloved children, and have clear understanding of our vision and destiny, so that we can follow our calling to move forward. For Your name's sake, You lift us up higher among multitudes when we reverentially fear You and humble ourselves and glorify Your name, so that many may be drawn to You.

Holy Spirit! Please help my family, that everyone in my family have Godly relationships with one another. Let men to be the overseers, to be above reproach, faithful to his wife, temperate, self-controlled, respectable, hospitable, and able to teach; not given to drunkenness, not violent but gentle; no quarrelsome, not a lover of money. He shall manage his own family well and see that his children obey him, and he must do so in a manner worthy of full respect (I Tim. 3:2-4); Also, fearing God with all his family; and he gives money to the poor, and make prayers to God at all times. (Act. 10:2), he keeps harmonious and unity among siblings, forgive each other. Women as wives submit to the husband just as submit to the Lord.

Holy Spirit! Please lead us to submit to the Lord, respect to the authorities that Lord has established, and refuse to rebel or slander. Keep us away of criticizing and judging others. Help us to trust in God and obey, teach us how to keep integrity and honesty, trust in Your deliverance and blessing. Help us care about the relationships we have with Father God, and healthy Godly relationships with others. Help us to walk with You all the time.

Father, Son and Holy Spirit! Grant us with Your promise, that You send ministering angels to surround our family to protect us, hide us under the shadow of your wings and help us to always dwell in Your secret place. You deliver us from the snares of the fowler and from the noisome pestilence. No evil will come on us, and no disease will come near our tent. We put our trust in You and by the strength You gave to us we will put our foot on the lions and the snake, the young lions and the great snake will be crushed under our feet.

You set us on high, You are with us when we are in trouble, You have shown us your salvation and blessings and satisfied us with long life. You have promised us that You are our provider, You supply all our needs and provisions, and help us to have Godly relationships with everyone You have given to us. Help us always remember that You are the source of our every provision, everything we have now were blessings from You, and offer you a sacrifice of thanksgiving always.

Help us to be the blessing vessels of my family, I proclaim in Jesus' name—Your grace is sufficient enough for me. I pray in thanksgiving and in Jesus' mighty name. Amen.

[Declaration of God's Promises]

Father God, thank you for your promises, scripture tells me: if I diligently obey the LORD my God, being careful to do all Your commandments which You command me today, the LORD my God will set me high above all the nations of the earth. [2]"All these blessings will come upon me and overtake me if I obey the LORD my God (Due. 28:1-2). How blessed is the man who does not walk in the counsel of the wicked, nor stand in the path of sinners, nor sit in the seat of scoffers! But his delight is in the law of the LORD, and in His law he meditates day and night. [3]He will be like a tree firmly planted by streams of water, which yields its fruit in its season and its leaf does not wither; and in whatever he does, he prospers. (Psalm 1:1-3) and if you belong to Christ, then you are Abraham's descendants, heirs according to promise. (Gal. 3:29).

Therefore, Father God, I choose to follow Your commandments, Your precepts. I choose the destiny and calling You have predestined for me and follow You. Thank You Father for sending Your only beloved Son Christ Jesus to cleanse all my sins and iniquities, and send the Holy Spirit our counselor, to lead me on the path of Your calling. Dear Holy Spirit, I choose to depend on You, please lead me daily, help me to acknowledge Him in all my ways.

I believe, I will receive all the blessings in the heavenly realm that Father has given to me in Christ Jesus, and all the promises and blessings of Abraham, and abundant life that Jesus has promised to us.

Father God! I believe, I will be blessed in the city, and blessed in the country. The fruit of my womb will be blessed, and the crops of my land and the young of my livestock—the calves of my herds and the lambs of my flocks. My basket and my kneading trough will be blessed. I will be blessed when I come in and blessed when I go out. The LORD will grant that the enemies who rise up against me will be defeated before us. They will come at me from one direction but flee from me in seven.

I believe the LORD will send a blessing on my barns and on everything I put my hand to. The LORD my God will bless me in the land he is giving me. The LORD will establish me as his holy people, as he promised me on oath, if I keep the commands of the LORD our God and walk in his ways. Then all the peoples on earth will see that I am called by the name of the LORD, and they will fear me. The LORD will grant me abundant prosperity—in the fruit of my womb, the young of my livestock and the crops of my ground—in the land he swore to my forefathers to give me. The LORD will open the heavens, the storehouse of his bounty, to send rain on my land in season and to bless all the work of my hands. I will lend to many nations but will borrow from none.

The LORD will make me the head, not the tail. If I pay attention to the commands of the LORD our God and carefully follow them, I do not turn aside from any of the commands Moses gave to us, to the right or to the left, following other gods and serving them. I will always be at the top, never at the bottom, and receive abundant blessings and grace from Father God. Amen.

[Daily Proclamation of God's Provision]

Father God! I give You all honor and praise, for You are my shepherd. I shall not want. You are Omnipotent, Omniscient, and Omnipresent God. You know all my needs. I believe that You will meet all our needs according to Your glorious riches in Christ Jesus. I belong to Jesus, I am in Him Who is Abraham's Seed, then I am Abraham's offspring and heirs according to promise.

I chose to follow Your command, Your will, precepts, and law. I faithfully offer my best and first fruit and glad tithing (the whole tenth of my income) into the storehouse, that there may be food in Your house. I am determined to honor (esteem and value as precious) my parents and accept them as who they are, and love them, and You promised me that all may be well with me and that I may live long on the earth. I chose to love one another, and be gracious to others and do not short of other's wages, be not stingy, nor get petty. The scripture says "It is more blessed to give than to receive" (Act 20:35) I give, and will be given to me; good measure, pressed down, shaken together, and running over, will they pour into [the pouch formed by] the bosom [of my robe and used as a bag]. For with the measure I deal out [with the measure I use when I confer benefits on others], it will be measured back to me. I seek first the Kingdom of God and righteousness;

Father God will supply all my need.

Therefore, I will plant seed as much as possible, treat others with generosity and tolerance. I remember the poor, God will remember me. I sow in time of famine, I will reap hundred fold in that very year. Grant me wisdom, oh Father God, so that I will sow on the good soil, and it will grow one hundred fold. Then You will rebuke the enemy of devourer on my behalf, thieves will be unable to touch my properties, and You will open the storehouse of heaven and pour down Your blessings on me, and my barns will be filled to overflowing, and my vats will brim over with new wine.

In Jesus' name I declare that I am favored by God. Father God, I set my love upon You, You will open the door of favor and blessings, and help me to receive all the Kingdom inheritance according to Your promises. Father God, thank You for giving me so much favor. Your favor is wonderful, mighty, abundant, supernatural, and shields me all around. Every day, Your favor and blessings fill me, surround me, pour unto me, and adding into my life unceasingly. Your favors open the door of financial abundance for me, and anoint me with the spirit of wisdom to be a good housekeeper for Kingdom finance, help me to be a faithful and good housekeeper for the Lord. Father God will assign me with more of His inheritance.

God blessed me on all the works of my hand, His glorious storehouse of heaven opened for me forever. I dwell in His glory of increase and multiplication. Because I am fellow heir and fellow member of the body, and fellow partakers of the promise in Christ Jesus through the gospel, I have unlimited access to all things in the Kingdom: all the gold and silver, and all the earthly abundance. I am blessed with every spiritual blessing in the heavenly places in Christ. I am blessed with all the blessings that pertain to life and to godliness. I am blessed when I come in and go out, the offspring of my body shall be blessed, the produce of my ground shall be blessed, and my job, career and income will all be blessed.

I open my heart, my spirit to receive my financial miracles. By faith I proclaim those unseen miracles to become true. My income will not stop flowing in. My bank account balance is more than enough. All my bills will be paid on time. All the loans paid off, debts cancelled. In Christ I have more than enough abundance, God has given me overflowing abundance. Lord Jesus, in Christ I have the power to make wealth, in You I accumulate inheritance for my children, in You I have secured future.

I labor with joy, diligence, and excellence in Your name and for Your glory. The hands of the diligent make rich. I proclaim the truth; I am rich because You reward the hands of the diligent. I love and embrace wisdom every day and therefore I experience riches, honor and fullness of life.

You make me a magnet of blessing, blessings will look for me. They come upon me and overtake me. When I shop, You make the way for me to receive unspeakable blessings. You create sales and discounts on my behalf. Whatever I need, You provide.

You grant me promotions and open new doors of favorable opportunities for me. You not only bless me but You make me a blessing. You show me daily how I can be a blessing to others. You grant me abundance so that I can sow into the Kingdom of God and lives of other individuals, ministries, and nations.

Harm will not touch me. Poverty and lack do not come near me. Recession shall not touch me. Failures in the world's economics system do not affect me or pertain to me for I am a Kingdom child. I only live in the blessing zone. I expect miracles of blessing to manifest daily because of Your faithfulness. I am of Kingdom people who live in Your abundance. I am forever blessed. I am forever thankful. I love You, Lord, with all my heart, mind and strength. I will serve You with joy and gladness all the days of my life. Thank You for Your unfailing love and goodness. Thank You for being more than enough. I love You, Jesus! Amen.

[Prayer for Marriage]

Lord Jesus, Please help _____(husband) and _____(wife) to know that being a husband and wife stands for a union, joint together which becomes an undivided one (Gen.2:24, Mark 10:7,9). Help us to trust You, that you are almighty God, no matter how we look or think of each other, You can always help us to know how to appreciate each other, love, understand and tolerate each other. Help us see each other's need, and be willing to fulfill marital duty to each other, to please each other and please God. (1 Cor. 7:3-34) Make our relationship established in Christ Jesus, with satisfactory fellowship. Teach us to know how to honor marriage, keep our devoir, submit to each other to obey Your command (Hebrew 13:4). Let the wife know how to respect and honor the husband, and the husband know how to love the wife as his own body, let us know how to keep our due responsibility to love each other and follow You.

Lord Jesus, I offer my marriage to You, please keep us in You. Give us patience, faithfulness, love and encouragement, and help us to imitate Lord Jesus that our attitude and behavior toward our family members be similar to how Christ Jesus will treat us (Rom. 15:5). Please help us and give us the greater love (agape love) as well as a renewed love for each other. Love suffers long and is kind; love does not envy;

67

love does not parade itself, is not puffed up; [5]does not behave rudely, does not seek its own, is not provoked, thinks no evil, does not calculative; [6]does not rejoice in iniquity, humble, does not compete, not strive to win, but rejoices in the truth; [7]bears all things, believes all things, hopes all things, endures all things. Make us love each other, honor each other, to speak truth in love and honoring, open and honest to each other, willing to listen and communicate with each other without criticism or judgment, and to respond to each other with ways that the spouse likes and is comfortable with, and with understanding and kind consideration, that we can appreciate and applause each other, honoring each other, and willingly commit to each other with heart, body, time and things , to rejoice each other, ignite and burn us to love each other with our life, remove any blockages in our relationships, so nothing can stop our love for each other.

Lord, please help us not to try and change each other, not to expect or demand things the other person can't give, not expect each other to be perfect, not to ask for unreasonable request. Help us not to communicate with our own method and ways with each other that include command, warning, threatening, or laws, virtues, counseling, logics, argu-ment and teaching, criticism, chastising, labeling, silence, anger, defenses, selfishness, withdrawal and questioning. Help us to choose to obey your command and treat each other according to Your will, let us chose to love, praise, appreciate, admire, agree, believe, trust, understand and forgive, and help us to remove any bitter root, or negativity, and over expectation, fear, resentment, self-center acts, criticisms, judgments, control, interrogation, doubt, pride, guilt, anger, hurt, and tiredness. Help us to be united in the Lord Jesus Christ, because of the love of the Lord. Please give me the love that You have for _____(name of the spouse) in my heart, help us to see each other through Your eyes, to see _____'s strength, and tolerate _____'s weakness, so we can share with each other to nurture and satisfy our spirit, soul and body.

[Prayer for Husband]

Lord Jesus! Please make (husband) be the spiritual head of the house, royal priest, as well as establish the family altar, teach the children and administrate his family with God's way. Make it so he covers his family with Godly prayers and blessing, he is willing to sacrifice himself for the wife, he loves his wife as his own body (Eph. 5:22-28), he will not mistreat his wife (Col. 3:19), the love he has for his wife is reinvigorated to the time when he first started loving his wife, his wife's bosom satisfy him always and may he ever be captivated by her love. Make it do he drinks water from his own cistern, running water from his own well (Prov. 5:15-19), He also in the same way be considerate as he lives with his wife, and treats his wife with respect, as the weaker partner and as heirs with him of the gracious gift of life, so that nothing will hinder his prayers. (1 Peter 3:7)

[Prayer for Wife]

Oh Lord Jesus! Please make it so (wife) submit, honor and respect her husband, she has holy behavior in the fear of God, she is clothed with strength and dignity; she speaks with wisdom, and faithful instruction on her tongue, she holds the inward adorning and beauty of the hidden person of the heart, with the incorruptible and unfading charm of a gentle and peaceful spirit, she does what is right without being frightened by any fear. (1Peter 3:1-7) (Eph. 5:33) (Prov. 31:10-31) Make it so she also is a woman worthy of respect, not a malicious talker but temperate and trustworthy in everything.(1 Tim. 3:11), she be reverent in the way she lives, not to be addicted to much wine, but to teach what is good, to love her husband and children, to be self-controlled and pure, to be busy at home, to be kind, and to be submissive to her husband, so that no one will malign the word of God.(Titus 2:3-5)

Lord Jesus, please keep my wife to be the crown of her husband (Prov. 12:4), the heart of her husband trusts in her, she is the glory of her husband (1 Cor. 11:7), an excellent woman (Prov. 12:4), a prudent wife

(Prov. 19:14) and a wise woman who builds her house (Prov.14:1). Make it so she does her husband good and not evil all the days of her life (Prov. 31:12), she has a reputation for good works, she brings up children, she shows hospitality to strangers, she washes the saints' feet, she assists those in distress, and she devotes herself to every good work. (1 Tim. 5:10)

Lord release grace and mercy among us, that we can quickly forgive each other and accept each other, honor each other, and plead the blood of Jesus and heal the wound we dealt to each other, so that the heart of (husband) turn to (wife) and (wife) will be satisfied in his love, and be willing to forgive and accept each other just as the Lord accepts and forgives us unconditionally. Both (husband) and (wife) will give up all the control and manipulation, truly consider each other whole heartedly, and love each other as love our own body.

In Jesus' name, I bind and command all the power of darkness that are disturbing our marriage to leave us, including all kind of, events, projects, evil spirit, witchcraft, voodoo, control, confusion, disappointment, misunderstanding, Jezebel spirit ...etc. In Jesus' name, I cancel all your work assignments, break all curses, all the evil plane that try to divide us, and declare it null and void, and no longer have any effect in our marriage. In Jesus' name, I proclaim that all the goodness, blessings, grace, acceptance, forgiveness, faithfulness, honesty, and honor will fall upon us, dwell in our marriage relationship, and we will love and honor each other to glorify our Lord Jesus and Father God in heaven. Amen.

[Prayer for Parents]

Father God, I thank You for my parents. I can grow up because they have tried their best to contribute into my life the love and sacrifices they knew best. They have taught me so that I did not go astray. Father God please remember their labor and bless them to have intimate relationship with You, so they can receive Your grace and the great plan of redemption.

Lord! Bless my parent with physical health. Keep them from any kind of illness, diseases or evil attacks or wound and trauma that tries to steal their years on earth. You are Jehovah Rapha, please heal all the weakness and afflictions of my parents, so that they can walk and move freely, with clear eye-sight and hearing ability, with full of joy, peace and hope.

Dear Lord, please fill my parents with the spirit of joy so that they will keep a joyful heart and never worry for their children. Please remove any gap in between the generations, and any domination and control or manipulation, heal our relationships in different generations. Teach my parent so they know how to come to you and cast all their burdens unto you, they will not worry or carry a heavy burden. Please keep their heart, release "shalom", supernatural peace to them, so that they will see that their children are their blessing and glory, they will see their children through Your eye and they will know Your will for their children. Lord! Please bless my parent, their heart will be satisfied when they see their children seek your face, and give You all the glory, and they will have no gap in their relationship with their children.

Lord, please help my parent that they will not feel lonely, God of Emmanuel, please help them to know that You are with them all the time, You send Your ministering angels to surround them, You keep and watch over them in and out, keep them safe in all their ways. You bless their human relationship, keep them away from all slanderers and bad company, lead them not into temptation and deliver them from all evil, give them wisdom to live a glorious life.

Lord, please help my parent so their relationship grows deeper and closer with each other, their word to each other are gentle and kind. Please heal and mend all the wounded and broken areas in their hearts with life. Lord! Please help them accept each other, understand and tolerate each other, give grace and mercy to each other, love each other until through old age. Lord, please wrap Your love around father and mother, use Your wondrous wisdom to lead them into the ways of eternal life. Heal and comfort their heart, let them know every storm they went through in their lives are not in vain, You will heal and restore no matter when it happened, everything they lost in life, opportunity, reputation, money, health, relationship, for You will comfort, guide, support and help them, use double blessings to restore them. You let all things work together for their good benefit; they are called by Your will, they will receive all the blessings in the heavenly place, also blessings of offspring of Abraham. In Jesus' name. Amen.

[Prayer for Children]

Dear Lord Jesus, You are our peace maker, please remove all the walls that hinders the relationships between my spouse and I. Help us to have like mindedness in the way of disciplining our children. Please fill our hearts with Your agape love, so that we may also unconditionally love _____ (name of children). Let our love for each other to be lively and exciting, that in tough and long suffering times, we may be graceful and kind, that we do not use control, domination or manipulation against each other. Let the discipline and nourishment we give to our child complement and complete to each other.

Lord, please release the special and perfect love that You have for every child in our heart, myself and my spouse. Help us to know how to treat every child, so that _____ will know he/she is special and unique, _____ has a special place in our heart, he/she has favor of his/her parents, that he/she is a tender boy/girl in front of father and the only son/daughter in front of the mother. Lord, help _____, to pay attention to what You say and listen closely to Your words, let them not leave the sight of _____, keep them within _____'s heart; help _____ to gain life and health to his/her body when he/she finds them (Prov. 4:2,20-22). Lord Jesus, please keep _____'s body healthy, give him/her a strong immune system, so that he/she suffers no illness or harm. Give _____ a healthy and strong body, thank You Jesus.

In Jesus name I bless _____ to grow in wisdom and stature, and in favor with God and men. Lord I ask that you will help _____ to have a gentle and humble heart, receive Your words, and treasure Your commands within him/her, incline his/her ear to wisdom, and apply his/her heart to understanding, discernment, and lift up his/her voice for understanding. Lord Jesus please help _____ to remember Your law, and keep Your commands; let not mercy and truth forsake him/her; bind them around _____'s neck, write them on the tablet of _____'s heart, and let him/her find favor and high esteem in the sight of God and man. Let _____ trust in the LORD with all his/her heart, and lean not on his/her own understanding; in all his/her ways acknowledge You, and please direct _____'s paths, and not be arrogant to his/her own wisdom. Let _____ fear the LORD and depart from evil, till the end of his/her life. (Prov. 2:1-2, 3:1-8)

Father God, Please help _____ to keep his/her heart with all diligence, help him/her to put away a deceitful mouth, put perverse lips far from _____. Let _____'s eyes look straight ahead, with righteousness. Let him/her ponder the path of his/her feet, and let all his/her ways be established. Do not turn to the right or to the left; and remove _____'s

77

foot from evil. Lord, please help _____ overcome the temptations of young men/women, help him/her to have Godly relationships with his/her friend.

Father God, please help _____ to accept his/her gender. Help and guide _____ in his/her growing process, also teach us to grow with them together. If we ever had expected _____ to be a different gender from how you created him/her, please forgive us and heal _____ so he/she can see himself/herself through Your eyes. Help _____ to know how to keep his/her body holy and sanctified for You and help _____ to follow Your command in the ways of relationship with those of opposite sex. Keep _____ from all temptations and snares. Father God please sent Your guardian angels to watch over _____ and protect him/her, let no evil weapon formed against _____ to prosper.

In Jesus' name I bless _____ to receive the prosperous blessings from Abraham, and receive the Holy Spirit that Father God has promised to us, let the wisdom that comes from above fall upon _____.I bless _____ to be the head not the tail, to be above and not beneath.Lord bless _____'s learning process to fulfill the calling and destiny that You have created him for, and also prepare his/her life partner to walk on the path of Kingdom, to build a family that can glorify the Lord. In Jesus' name. Amen.

[Prayer for Unsaved Family Members]

Lord Jesus! There is no other name under heaven given to men by which _____ (name of unsaved family members) can be saved. Thank You for Your promise that if one within the family is saved, then the whole family may receive Your grace, thank You for the price that You, Lord Jesus, has paid for us that my whole family now has hope to receive your grace and salvation. When I believe in Lord Jesus, my family and I will be saved. It's by Father's grace that I am saved, not because of my good works. Have mercy on me, Oh Lord, although I have not been able to live a life like Jesus yet, I ask that You release Your great love, for You are rich in mercy. Revive my family so we may be with Christ even though we were dead in our transgressions.(Eph. 2:4) I believe that the power of Holy Spirit who is moving in my life and has led me into salvation, can also move on and surround my family members, so that they too can be saved.

Have mercy upon _____(name unsaved family members), they may be blinded, deceived, bound by the enemy. Please release Your mighty power to open the eyes of _____'s heart, that has been blinded by the god of this world, so that _____ can repent and truly know You. Please place the power of the blood and cross in between _____ and all the powers of darkness that hinders them. Make it so that all the things of this world, family member, relatives, friends, traditions, value and anything that exalts flesh will not be able to stop them to be baptized in Jesus' name. (Act. 4:12)

Oh Lord! How I pray that You are also the God of my _____ (parents/ brothers, sisters/spouse/son, daughter), be the God of my whole family. I pray for the relationships between You and my family members, please give _____ wisdom from above to receive salvation that You have given to us through Jesus Christ. In Jesus name I bind all the power of darkness behind _____(name of the unsaved one) and cancel all the assignments of enemy's tactics. In Jesus' name I declare that all the high things that exalts self which is blocking _____ to know Jesus shall all tumble down under the power of God, so his/her heart will all be set free, return to Jesus and surrender to Him.

In Jesus' name I bind all evils powers that are blocking _____ to receives the Truth of salvation and break the power of all strong holds in (his/her) mind that came from the traditional culture and religion (Buddhism, Taoism, Confucianism, Muslim, Communism, worshiping ancestors or the dead...etc.) Lord, I ask you reveal the Truth in their heart, let the light of the Truth shine and flood their minds eye so he/she can understand that You are the only one true God. Jesus is the Way, Truth and Life. In Jesus' name I pray. Amen.

[Prayer offering of Thanksgiving]

Thank You, Lord, I believe that the wholeness of Holy Spirit will break the yoke of my family line and all our heavy burdens will depart from our shoulders. (Isaiah 10:27). Thank You, Lord, that Your anointing remove all our heavy burdens and release the garment of praise. Thank You Lord, Your anointing brings in your glorious beauty to replace the ashes in our life.

Thank You Lord, that Holy Spirit will reveal the Truth for my Family, The Truth who is not just philosophy, but a person, He has a wonderful name, His name is above all names, His name is Jesus Christ; He is the Way, The Truth and The Life. In His great and mighty name, I declare, Jesus will manifest in every area of our life.

Lord, thank You. That Your anointing will restore and renew the generational ruins of my family line. You are restoring all that the enemy has robbed from us. Your blessings endure forever. Your word will not go in vain; You always complete what You have willed for us.

For as many as are the promises of God, we all find their Yes [answer] in You [Jesus Christ]. For this reason we also say "Amen" (so be it) to God through You [in Your Person and by Your agency] to the glory of God. Amen.

[Prayer for Pastors, Ministers in church]

✝   Lord Jesus, we thank you for you have called pastor and ministers and their spouses to serve in Your kingdom. Thank those that have answered Your call in their free will, served us as though as serving You, with all their heart, all their will and all their strength.

✝   Lord, You are holy and righteous, full of compassion, love and mercy. Lord I ask that you bless our Pastor and ministers and their spouses to be holy and pure hearted in all things, so that they can see you face to face. Father God of our Lord Jesus Christ, Father of glory, grant our pastors and ministers and their spouses the Spirit of wisdom and revelation, so their knowledge of You will be increased, enabling them to receive fresh revelations from you, and have a close intimate relationship with You, so they can build a glorious church together with all the saints, to prepare for Your second coming.

✝   Lord Jesus, I pray that You will draw our pastors and ministers and their spouses near to you. When they are close to You, You will be even closer to them. I pray that You pour Your love into their hearts, let them truly experience the height, the width, the length and depth and unlimited agape love You have for them.

✝   Lord Jesus, I pray that You will help our

pastors and ministers and their spouses to have and maintain quality time with You, be hungry to know You more in personal ways, and have suitable places for their devotion time. In Jesus' name we rebuke and command all evil powers that distract and hinder them from a close relationship with the Lord, commanding each and every power/spirit to leave and come out of them, right now!

✞   You make them lie down and rest in Your bosom. Soak them in Your River of living water. Lord, renew their strength that they shall mount up with wings as eagles; they shall run, and not be weary; and they shall walk and not faint. You anoint them with fresh oil, let their cup runes over. You lead them and have them gather strength to strength, grace to grace, and glory to glory.

✞   Lord Jesus! I pray that You bless our pastors and ministers and their spouses to prosper in every way, including a healthy and able body, just as their soul keep well and prosper. (3rd John 1:2).Lord Jesus, I pray that You bless our pastors and ministers and their spouses to glorify You in all things, whether they eat or drink, or whatever they may do. Grant them Your wisdom, joy and peace, so that they can walk with You under any and all kinds of circumstances. In all their ways know, recognize, and acknowledge You, and You will direct and make straight and plain their paths, and let their ways be a delight in Your sight, so that they be blessings to many.

✝   Lord Jesus, I pray that You bless our pastors and ministers and their spouses to always have reverential fear of You, not fear of man or evil, and continuously receive visions and revelations from You. Release the Spirit of counsel to them, show them Your strategy, tactics, methods, timing, and people that You have chosen. We ask that You grant our pastors and ministers and their spouses wisdom from above, so they will know how to prioritize their time according to Your order and priority. Make them be always sensitive to the prompting of the Holy Spirit, sensitive to the works You are doing on things, people and events that surround them. Make it so that they are willing to pay the price to co-work with You, enjoy the fruit of Your work, and have favor from all co-workers, congregations and people they meet wherever they go.

✝   We ask that You release the spirit of unity in our church. Help each one of us to have one heart, one mind, be moved by one Spirit to follow You, follow the same vision that You have given us, help us to discard a deceitful mouths, perverse lips, focus on You, keep our eyes on You, and follow You.

✝   We ask that you anoint our pastors and ministers and their spouses with Your Spirit, so that they will preach the gospel to the poor, heal the sick, set the captives free, is a wise leader, so that all the saints in the congregation will obey Your command and follow Your great commission, and make all nations Your disciples.

✞   May all the glory, honor and all praise be unto the Lord. Lord Jesus, please lead not our pastors and ministers and their spouses into temptation and deliver them from all evil. In Jesus' name I command all criticisms, judgments and ungodly expectations to leave them and the church. Lord, come destroy and remove all these evil powers, that they do not prosper over our pastors, ministers and their spouses.

✞   Lord Jesus, I pray that the verse "the spiritual man tries all things [he examines, investigates, inquires into, questions, and discerns all things] "to become reality in the life of our pastors and ministers and their spouses, so that they can discern between truth and lies, and they will not be cheated by any lies from the enemy. Hide them under Your wings that they can lean on You, stand firm, against the enemy and be more than just an overcomer!

✞   Lord Jesus, You are our provider, I pray that You provide our pastors and ministers and their spouses with all their need. Make it so that they know how to use the resources You have provided for them

85

in the priority according to Your Kingdom order. Help them receive all your blessings, and that they will always seek Your Kingdom first. All the things they need, You shall surely add unto them. They will rejoice in the abundance You give to them and they will also be able to discern what comes from You and have clean hands to enjoy Your richness without worry.

✝   Lord Jesus, please bless our pastors and ministers and their spouses to be a Godly husband, father, son or daughter, wife, mother, and any kind of role they have in their life. They are blessings to others and to manifest Your glory in all of these roles. Let there be no longer any wanting to those who truly revere and worship Him with godly fear. When they serve You with all their heart, You surround them and their family members and relatives with shield of grace to protect them, they shall have no worry or anxiety. In Jesus' name. Amen.

[Faith Declaration of Receiving God's Healing]

(Note: Please pray the Lordship prayer; invite Jesus Chris to be the Lord of every area, and every moment of your life, and ask Him to be the Lord of every cell, DNA and RNA and every particle of your spirit, soul and body. Also invite Holy Spirit to fill, and saturate, and permeate every cell, unit, DNA and particle of your spirit, soul and body.)

Father God, I thank You, For I know the thoughts and plans that You have for me, are the thoughts and plans for welfare and peace and not for evil, to give me hope in my final outcome (Jeremiah 29:11). The God and Father of our Lord Jesus Christ (the Messiah) has blessed us in Christ with every spiritual (given by the Holy Spirit) blessing in the heavenly realm! Even as [in His love] He chose us [actually picked us out for Himself as His own] in Christ before the foundation of the world, and lavished all these blessings upon us in every kind of wisdom and understanding (practical insight and prudence) (Eph. 1:3-8).

Thank You, Father God, You sent Your only begotten Son, Jesus Christ to me, He became my sin offering, He shed His precious blood for me and cleansed all my sins. *He was* wounded for my transgressions, He was bruised for my iniquities; the chastisement for my peace was upon Him, and by His stripes I am healed.

87

Because of the redemptive work Jesus complete on the cross, I can reconcile with You, I can come back home to Father God's house, and be adopted as Your child. Jesus Christ in the body of His flesh through death, presented me as holy, and blameless, and above reproach in Your sight and I can come boldly to the throne of grace, that I may obtain mercy and find grace to help in time of need.

Father God, thank You for your abundant grace and mercy, and every promise You have for us in Christ, and all these promises I say "Yes and Amen" in Jesus Christ. I want to receive all these promises. I declare that by the Lord who gave me all power, I can receive all the promises that Father God promised.

Now, in the name of Jesus Christ, by the power of the blood and cross, and by the guidance of the Holy Spirit, I come before Your throne of grace, to obtain mercy and find grace to help me in time of need, I come to obtain promises You have promised.

Thank You for promising to forgive all my iniquities and heal all my diseases, You redeem my life from destruction, and crown me with loving kindness and tender mercies. You satisfy my mouth with good things, So that my youth is renewed like the eagle's (Psalm 103:5). Your word says that "For as the heavens are high above the earth, so great is His mercy toward those who fear Him; As far as the east is from the west, so far has He removed our transgressions from us. Thank You Father, You are merciful, and gracious abounding in love. Thank You Father, for You are faithful and just, if I confess my sins, You are faithful and just to forgive all my sins and cleanse me from all unrighteousness.

Father, I confess, my ancestors and my family and I have sinned against You. We rebelled against You, and we have forsaken You, the fountain of living waters. We have done evil, each gone our own way; therefore iniquities, death, disasters fall upon us. We used other gods and replaced You, therefore our sorrow multiplies. Please forgive us for all these sins and cleanse us from all these unrighteousness. Forgive us for we did not love You our God with all our heart, all our mind, all our will, we did not love our neighbors as our self; we did not follow Your commands and precept, so that we allowed curses to followed us and catch us. Please also forgive us for we did not take good care of our body, the temple of Holy Spirit, and also abused our body, please forgive us for all these sins, and cleanse us from all unrighteousness.

Now, as You forgive and cleanse us, I also choose to forgive everyone who has hurt my family, my ancestors, and myself and release them into the freedom of my forgiveness. If any member of my family member and ancestors have hurt anyone due to our decisions and deeds, please also forgive us. Please also forgive me for any secret unknown sin. I bless everyone and there family members and offspring, bless every one of them so they can receive the abundant life You have promised us in Jesus Christ. I also choose to forgive myself, accept myself according to the way that You have forgiven me and accepted me. I choose to love myself as You loved me, and choose to receive the long, wide, deep and high love that You have given to me in Jesus' Christ.

Now, In Jesus' name!! I declare that I have received the law of life and Spirit, I am free from the law of sin and death. Jesus has taken the curses for me on the cross, I am entering into blessing and have been freed from all curses. Jesus became poor for me, that I may receive the abundant life that He has promised to me. Jesus has wiped out the handwriting of requirements that was against me, which was contrary to me, He has taken it out of the way, and nailed it to the cross. Now I declare "By His stripe, I was healed, all the symptoms of all diseases and pain on my body, are healed. In Jesus' name, I sever the spirit, soul and body linking between me and everyone that I have forgiven and all the ancestors of my father's family line and my mother's family line. In Jesus' name, I command all the spirits related to diseases, infirmity, affliction, fear, terror, pain, death, destruction, oppression, heaviness, despair, grief, sorrow, trauma, accident, curses, unbelief, lies, bitterness, hatred, rejection, separation, rebellion, accusation, self-condemnation... all go out of me, never to return, never to hurt any human beings.

In Jesus' name, I also break all the curses related to _____(name of diseases for example: heart disease, cancer, arthritis, diabetes, high blood pressure, blind, deaf, scoliosis, allergy, trauma, accident...etc.), and all the self-made curses, inner vows that my ancestors, my family members and myself had made, and any agreement and covenant that we had made with the enemy, I declare them as null and void, they no longer can affect me. In Jesus' name, I command all evil spirits related to _____(these/this disease/s) to go out of me, never to return, never to disturb anyone else. If there are any ancestral spirits that have been bonded and is influencing me, due to the sin of ancestral worship, I commit you into the hand of Jesus Christ, you can go in peace to where Jesus sends you to go. Father God, send holy angels to help me complete all the prayers I have made.

In Jesus' name, I plead the precious blood of Jesus Christ, to cleanse me, wipe away all the evil marks that the enemy left in my spirit, soul and body due to any unrevealed sin. I ask Father God to seal these areas with the seal of redemption, sanctify these areas and give unto the Lord God Almighty, our Father in heaven. (Pause, and be quiet... meditate and imagine that the power of blood of Jesus Christ now flowing through every part of your person, every cell, every particle, let His sanctifying power of the blood merge into every cell and every particle of your being)

Father God, I thank You and praise You, the Lord is the portion of my cup, and my inheritance. My body is the temple of the Holy Spirit, the spiritual house that has been built by You. Father God I pray that the power of life and resurrection of my Lord Jesus Christ now come and fill every cell, every molecule of my body, and permeate me. Thank you Father God, for how great is your manifestation of power on those who believe. This great power is the power that worked wonders through Jesus, the power that caused Jesus to revive from the dead is within me, flowing in my life, flowing into every cell and molecule.

Life and resurrection overcomes death and diseases; light overcomes darkness; blessing overcomes curses; truth overcomes lies; I was dead within my sin, now I have resurrected with Jesus Christ, and am seated in the heavenly place with Him together. The Church is the body of Christ, the fullness of Him who fills all in all. I am one part of Church, also one part of the body of Christ, that You also fill all in all. I welcome You, Father God. Come, now. Come and fill me up, let my spirit, soul, body be filled by Your rich treasury and glory, I can live out a life destined to glorify your name, manifest Your abundant life and lift up all glory and honor and praises to You! In Jesus' name. Amen.

In the name of Jesus, I command all of the cells in my body, especially _____ (name the parts that are sick, for example: blood, lungs, joints, intestines, stomach, immune system...etc.) Now realign in the order of God's creation, returning me to the glory of God's image and likeness. (If you know what healthy condition your body should return to, declare it, such as "My blood pressure is 120/80, my cholesterol index under 180 etc.", if you are not clear about it, you don't need to declare, just trust in the work of the Lord.) Amen.

[Declaration for Health (Myself, friend or relatives)]

If the prayer is for yourself, change the underlines and pronouns to first person

[Decree of Breaking the Power of Disease]

In the name of Jesus Christ I decree! Jesus is the Lord and savior of _____'s (name of the person) life, because Jesus was crucified for _____'s sin, He was wounded for our transgressions, He was bruised for our iniquities; and suffered pains of punishment.

In Jesus's name, I declare that Jesus has already forgiven all the sins of _____, heal all the diseases of _____. _____ has heavenly health, any sickness or pain has no power or right over _____. _____ has been forgiven, by His wound, _____ was healed. In Jesus' name, I decree _____ renounce and break all accusations and lies from all powers, including the power of principalities, the rulers of the darkness of this age, and spiritual hosts of wickedness in the heavenly places.

In the name of Jesus Christ, we declare _____ is over-comer. Jesus has victory over the world, flesh and the devil. He arrested all enemies and destroyed the ruler of death when He was resurrected. He made

94

_____overcome because of the blood of the lamb and our testimonies.

In the name of Jesus Christ I declare! He bore our grief (sicknesses, weaknesses, and distresses) and carried our sorrows and pain of punishment. _____declare that Jesus is the Lord of the spirit, soul, and body of _____. _____ reject all the pain and diseases to disturb _____'s body and declare, by the great power of Life and the resurrection, for the river of Life flow into _____. Every cell, gene, tissue, and organ of _____ receive healing power of the Lord and be restored back to the Lord's original created order.

[Decree Bible and Pray all the time] -Let Word of God Become Spiritual Food for your Daily Life.

Thank You Father, for You have given _____ abundant life, Word which is food of life, so that whenever _____listens to Your Word, pay attention to the scripture, in memory of your command and kindness and do not let Your Word apart from our eyes, _____ will receive life and gain health. Thank You, God for pouring Your life in _____'s heart, You set _____'s spirit, soul and body free. You made _____ love You, my Lord with all my (his/her) heart, all my (his/her)mind, and all my (his/her) will and also love my(his/her) neighbor, You helped _____ to forgive others, just like Christ

95

has forgiven _____. You made the spirit, soul and body of _____ harmonious, no more bitterness, grudges and inward battles. Father God, according to Your Word, _____ offer my(his/her) body to You as a living sacrifice, it's holy, and delights in You. (Rom. 12:1) In Jesus name, _____ declare that everything in _____, shall praise the Lord. In Jesus' name, _____ declares, everything in _____that does not come from God has been dissolved and removed. With the Word of the Lord that has been planted in every cell, _____can receive a Godly life. Disaster and plagues will not come near _____'s dwelling. For the Lord shall give His angels charge over _____, to keep _____in all _____'s ways. In the way of righteousness, life, healing and health.

[Tumor]

In Jesus' name, I declare that all the curses from the strike placed upon Egypt, the tumors, scab, and itch, from which you cannot be healed was completely broken on the cross. In Jesus' name I command all the tumors and cancer cells *(Please say out loud the tumors and the type of cancer that influencing you right now)* be dissolved and disappear, and leave _____'s body, without any residuals remaining, never to return or disturb any one in my family line. Jesus already died for me and my parents, ancestors, all the inequities and sins in my family line have been forgiven. I declare that the power of Life and Resurrection of Jesus Christ is moving inside of my body through the mighty power of the Holy Spirit our God now, dissolve all the tumors and cancer cells and restore _____'s strength and health.

In Jesus' name, _____ decree. Every organ and system of _____ was created by God, our creator. Every cell and organ must align with the will of Father God and operate according to His will and system. In Jesus' name, I command every cell and organ of _____'s body to be restored back to its original state, the state God created order and likeness, operates to His will and command until the day of completion according to the Father's will and time for _____ return to home in heaven.

[Cardiology and Blood Diseases]

(Use *"Cancel and break of blood /and covenant curse of generational line prayer"* first to break all the blood vows and covenant that ancestors had made with devil)

Thank You Jesus for the Precious blood you shed for _____, I now plead the blood of Jesus Christ over _____'s entire cardiovascular system, to erase off all the evil marks that enemies had left through curses.

I declare the power of life and resurrection to flow through _____'s blood and blood vessel and every cell in _____'s body, bring life into _____, and restore _____'s health. In Jesus' name we declare, _____obey all the teachings of Jesus Christ and choose to forgive everyone who have hurt _____, and also chose to give up all the bitterness, hatred and resentment, depression and frustration. _____ is determined to rejoice in the Lord despite any circumstances. Father God! Whenever _____ decree Your Word, the law of the Spirit of life in Christ Jesus made _____ free from the law of sin, curse and death. The river of living water flow in _____ and makes every cell filled with the power of life. A merited heart become medicine for _____'s body.

Thank You, Father! You filled _____'s heart with all the joy and peace, and made _____ full of hope through the power of Holy Spirit (Rome 15:13), thank You for pouring out the joyous anointing oil upon _____'s heart, healing and restoring _____'s cardio-vascular system from all damages. _____ is full of hope, because of the power of Holy Spirit and the river of living water, I believe when _____ is filled by Your joy, _____ will surely receive the grace of Your healing.

Oh! The Lord of host, You are _____'s strength and rock. You created a strong heart, You made _____'s heart beats follow the rhythm of life, You made _____'s blood flow into every cell, nurturing and restoring _____'s health and back to a harmonious stage.

Abba Father! Thank You for keeping _____'s blood pressure within a normal range, You made _____'s blood vessel elastic and full of life; the blood vessels moves and function properly. In Jesus' name, I command all the HDL in _____ to generate all the functions to remove all the clogs in the blood stream, so that all the plaque, and triglycerides (fat in blood) in the blood restores to a normal condition, every blood vessel and micro blood vessel passage shall remain clear, and cause _____'s blood pressure to remain normal and keep blood supplies in the body function normal. In Jesus' name I decree all stroke, blood vessel clog, and contractions depart from _____, never return or disturb anyone else.

In Jesus' name I command all the bacteria, virus, parasites spirochetes in _____ body that causes cardio-vascular diseases, die and disappear and leave _____ immediately, never to return or influence anyone. In Jesus' name I declare, _____ belongs to Jesus Christ, all the organs and cells that produce blood, Cardio system, Urinary system, Endocrine system to function well according to created order. _____ has been redeemed, and made _____ free from all the curses under the law.

Thank You Father, for the law of life and Spirit is flowing in _____, wash away all defilements and diseases in _____'s blood, and synchronize the heart beats of _____with the rhythm of life and set _____free.

[Immune System]

Thank You, Father God! You made it so _____'s immune system function properly, and is able to discern harmful bacteria, viruses and spirochetes, so that _____can be free of any attacks which can develop tumors, cancer-cells, arthritis, damage immune systems and microbiologic cells. No harmful bacteria and viruses can afflict _____.

Thank You for Your redemption, for You have power of living water, so that all the immune system in _____ can function normally, free from all attacks of diseases, pain, anxiety and death. In Jesus' name, I command all material, curses, evil spirits, power of darkness related to immune system disease to leave _____, because the power of life that resurrected Jesus from death lives in the _____'s spirit, soul and body, through the power of living water, the wisdom of the all mighty God synchronized _____'s immune system with Godly order, the law

100

of life and Spirit moving in _____'s body making _____'s immune system healthy and whole.

[Liver]

Oh! Lord God! I thank You, You have promised me, when _____trust in You and not lean on _____'s own understanding, In all ways _____acknowledge You, and You shall direct _____paths, having reverential fear of the Lord, depart from evil, You shall heal _____'s navel, and be nurturing to _____'s bone. (Prov. 3:5-8). Dear heavenly Father, You know all the causes of liver diseases. Please guide me and show me the cause of the disease in _____'s liver, help _____ to be totally free from any viruses/bacteria causing Hepatitis and contaminations, direct _____'s path, make _____depart away from all the acute or chronic hepatitis, tumor, and toil, grant _____ proper sleep, rest and food, help _____not to lean on _____in vain, but trust in You, have fear of Your wisdom, praise and bless and honor Your name, the way You prepared for _____is easy, and light. Help _____ focus only on You, seeking and fearing You, and loving You, You will surely heal _____'s navel, liver and all the bones according to Your promises. Oh Lord! _____praise You! Thank You for Your promises, when we trust in You, lean on You, and You heal _____, You embrace _____! Oh! Father!

_____ trust in You, lean on You and You alone, seek Your face only. Lord! Thank You for the healing grace flowing in the navel and bones of _____, You forgive all the sins of _____, and healed _____, made _____ whole.

In Jesus' name, I command all the viruses that cause liver cancer to leave _____, the materials that cause extra burdens to the liver to disappear, the tumor cells dissolve and disappear; every cell, tissue and function of _____'s liver restored back to original created order and likeness. Thank You for pouring the healing power on _____, You made _____'s liver whole and healthy. Thank You for loving us, I pray with thanksgiving and in the name of Jesus. Amen.

[Digestive, Elementary System]

Father God, I thank You for creating a healthy digestive, elementary system for me. Please forgive me and my ancestors for not following the Law of food You have given to us. We have turned against You to worship other gods, eaten food that were offered to idols, eaten blood as well the foods and medicine that You have forbidden us from eating. Please forgive us of all our iniquities and cleanse us from all unrighteousness. In Jesus name I break all power of evil effects and curses which come from theses

102

ungodly things we have eaten. I also chose to forgive everyone who had prepared and/or manufactured these foods and materials. As well as those who have invited me to attend feasts and festival of idols. I release each and every one of them into the freedom of my forgiveness. I acknowledge all curses of disaster, catastrophes, famine, draught, hunger, thirst, nakedness, and the need of everything due to the worship of other gods that also caused weakness and afflictions on my digestive system. I choose to forgive every ancestor who has brought me these afflictions, and release them into the freedom of my forgiveness. In Jesus' name, I break all curses and weaknesses in my digestive system, and declare them null and void, no longer will affect me. I plead the blood of Jesus unto my whole digestive, elementary system, cleanse and sanctify every cell, gene, DNA, erase all the evil marks that the devil made through the generational iniquity of my family lines, and restore every cell and molecule, gene back to original image and likeness of which Father God has created me with. In Jesus' name, I command _____ (speak out the area being affected by diseases) to receive the mighty healing power from Father God, and to be restored back to the original image and likeness that the Father created. I declare _____(your name and the weak part) by the wound of Jesus I am healed. In Jesus' name. Amen.

[Respiratory System and Allergy]

Father God, thank You for You have given me a healthy respiratory system. I confess for my ancestors, my family and myself have been burning incense in the temple of idols and/or have been addicted to opium/nicotine. We sinned against You defiling and damaging our respiratory system as well as bringing curses, knife and sword, war and war effect, disasters, catastrophes, flood, suicide by hanging, trauma, accident and death into our life all of which caused weakness of our lung, bronchi, and nose. Please forgive us of all these sins and cleanse us of all unrighteousness. I also chose to forgive every ancestor who has brought us all these weaknesses, and those people who have hurt my ancestors; I release each and every one of them into the freedom of my forgiveness. If my ancestors have ever hurt anyone who brought curses to my family, please forgive us, and cleanse us. Now in Jesus' name, I bless every one of them and their family offspring that was hurt by my ancestor or family, I bless them to know the salvation of Jesus Christ, and to receive and obtain the abundant life that the Lord Jesus promised. In Jesus' name I now break all respiratory weaknesses and curses and declare them null and void, no longer can affect me. In Jesus' name I command every evil spirit related to all these weaknesses and diseases to go out of me, go where Jesus wants you to go, never to return, never to hurt anybody else. Father God I ask You to release Your mighty healing power into my respiratory system, heal every tissue, cell, molecule, gene, in all my air ducts, lung and nose. Restore them back to original way Father God created. In Jesus' name, I command _____ (speak out the area being affected by diseases) to receive the mighty healing power from Father God, and be restored back to the original image and likeness that Father created. I declare _____ (your name and the weak part) by the wound of Jesus I am healed. In Jesus' name. Amen.

[Bone diseases \ Arthritis]

In Jesus' name, I declare, The Lord God will guard the feet of His saints, but the wicked shall be silent in darkness. (1 Samuel 2:9) Jesus was crucified on the cross, and all his bones were out of his joints, he bore all the curses of my joints and bones (Psalm 22:14). Father God, I thank You that You have promised to heal all of (name)'s diseases. (Psalm 103:3) In Jesus name, I decree, by Jesus' wound _____ is healed, I command all diseases, pain, cramp, damage and all evil power related to Arthritis (including Rheumatoid arthritis, Osteoarthritis, Psoriatic arthritis, Hypertrophic Osteoarthropathy, Septic arthritis, Gout, Ankylosing spondylitis, Inflammatory arthritis, …etc.) to go out of _____, never to return, never to hurt anyone else. Lord Jesus. I ask for the power of living water to pour in and fill every cell, every corner and every area of _____'s body. Release healing power into all damaged and painful areas of _____'s joints (say out loud those painful areas). Holy Spirit please continue Your works, pour in and smear Your mighty healing power upon _____. I pray for the blood of Jesus Christ to completely cover the immune system, autonomic nervous system, disc, and fluid of all the joints. Every cell every joint, disc, immune system, and autonomic nervous system shall restored back to the original likeness that Father God have created for _____. So that immune system disorder or function or whether change can not affect _____. _____shall be able to rejoice in the Lord with dancing and worship.

[Kidney Disease \ Urinary Tract system Diseases]

Father God, thank You for healing _____, so _____shall be healed, You save _____, so _____shall be saved, for You are _____'s praise (Jeremiah 17:14). Oh, Lord! I praise You, thank You for Your unconditional love, Your love is so wide, so long and so high and so deep. You have saved _____. I cast all _____'s burden to You, and hand all the pain, infirmities, suffering, excretion of unbalanced ion body fluid, waste and detoxification,

106

over to Your hand. Thank You for delivering _____ from *(name of disease)* and delivering _____completely from all the weakness of spirit, soul, and body caused by this disease. When I pray, I believe with all my heart, that the power of Your word has strengthened me. Thank You for granting me with merry heart, with which became good medicine for _____, so that _____ can receive heavenly healing and restoration and receive miraculous healing. Oh! Lord, I thank You for the guidance of the Holy Spirit and wisdom from above, so that _____ will know how to choose proper food for the present conditions of _____'s physical body. Please make it so that all the urinary fluid that is being filtered by the glomerulus is returned to normal, all the Proteinuria, chemical residues, body fluids, and electrolyte, PH level, and endocrine system function be restored back to the original created order that You made for _____. Father God! I believe that Your divine healing power is touching _____'s kidney, body fluid, urinary system right now. The living water that flows from Your throne is flowing through every kidney cell as well as nephron. In Jesus' name, I declare that all the functions of _____'s glomerulus has been restored.

_____'s body can now efficiently digest, his/her body now has a normal functioning metabolism which absorbs all nutrients, gets rid of all the waste, and has been completely healed. I pray all this in the victorious name of Jesus Christ. Amen.

[Prayer of Seeking Medical Help]

Father God! Please help _____ to completely depend on You to find a doctor and hospital, not to lean only to _____'s own understanding, I believe You will guide all our/my paths (Prov. 3:5-6). Thank You for preparing a good doctor for _____. When _____ receives medical help or surgery, please aid all the doctors and medical staff involved so they can have a clear mind, and can receive all the grace and wisdom from You. So they can make right decisions and judgments, so we can all receive Your abundant grace and healing power. Let us not receive only Your healing power and grace, but also receive abundant blessings and be able to enjoy Your glorious presence during the Godly process of healing through all the anointed doctors and staffs.

Lord Jesus! I ask that You bless every medical staff who is ministering to _____, also forgive every staff member for all ungodly influences they have that may negatively affect _____. In Jesus' name, I break and cut all the spirit, soul and body links between all evil spirit and human spirit, soul and body. I cancel all assignments of all rulers, and powers of darkness and evil spirits in heavenly places, so that they cannot influence or afflict harm

108

on _____ through medicine, or during the process of examination, diagnosis, or treatments. I pray, Oh Lord, that You also bless and sanctify all the medicines and drugs used in _____'s every treatment. Father God, I ask that You place the power of cross in between _____ and all powers of darkness to stop all ungodly flow. When the medical staff take blood from _____ for blood work, please bring back every part life of _____'s life that was contained in _____'s blood. If _____ need to receive a blood transfusion, please remove all ungodly elements in the blood being received and return all life that belongs to the donor back to him/her, so that all things work together for _____'s good, who loves God.

In Jesus' name, I command all evil spirit hiding under the pretense of healing, alternative healing, or good health, a cover for witchcraft, cult, defilement, addiction, meditation, acupuncture, Chi-gung, yoga, new life healing method...etc, I command you to cease all your activities and go out of _____, go where Jesus takes you, never to return and never to influence any other human being. Father God, please arrange all proper Western or Eastern healing methods and doctors for _____that is pleasing in Your sight. That You also send warrior angels to surround _____ during the process of treatment, protect him/her. Father God, I ask that You open the door of medical staff's hearts, so that we can be a blessing vessel for them, grant them with love, patience and encouragement during every process of medical treatment, also help _____ to become more and more Jesus Christ-like.

Lord Jesus! We firmly trust in You, we believe Your faithfulness and kindness is always with _____. Thank You for Your guidance during the whole process of medical treatment, healing, and caring. Please guard _____'s heart and mind, so that *he/she* can receive the grace of life fully, also let Your name be glorified through the entire healing process.

[Healthy Life]

I declare in Jesus' name, _____'s body is the temple of Holy Spirit, every part of _____'s body from head to toe, the living water of the Holy Spirit overflows from his/her body. All symptoms of _____ *(name of disease)* on _____'s body is totally healed. By the wounds of Jesus, _____ is totally healed, healing from the living water has flowed through every part and every cell of _____. Make it so _____ remain healthy.

In Jesus' name, I cancel every attack from microbiologic, organism and evil spirits, and declare them null and void, there is no trace of them in _____'s body, everything that is in _____'s body, shall praise the Lord!

The body of _____ is healthy and strong, no diseases and pain will prosper, because _____ depends and leans on the Lord God almighty.

Father God! Thank You for forgiving all _____'s iniquities, and heal all _____'s diseases, redeem _____'s life from destruction, crown _____ with loving kindness and tender mercies, and satisfy _____'s mouth with good *things*, so that _____'s youth is renewed like the eagle's. Father God! Thank You! _____ has already received all these blessings that You have granted to *him/her. He/she* has received life and health. I give all the glory of these miraculous turn around and break through unto You. May all the blessings and honor and glory be to the Lord forever and ever. Amen.

[Prayer of Joy]

Lord Jesus! Thank you for showing me the path to life. Coming before you, I have contentment and joy. You have eternal pleasures in your right hand. (Psalm 16:11) Thank you that I may rely on you for my joy, and you have told me to rejoice in you. (Philippians 4:4). A cheerful heart is good medicine, but a crushed spirit dries up the bones. (Proverbs 17:22) For the joy of the Lord is my strength. (Nehemiah 8:10) Thank you for giving me your words, I choose to rely on your might and power, choosing the abundant life you have given me. I refuse to let the enemy steal my fruit of joy. Please strengthen my heart, help me to live in your joy and grace every hour and every moment.

Lord Jesus! I choose to release my difficulties to you. Please work within me. I know I cannot overcome by my own strength, but I know I can rely on you through all of the difficulties in life and still remain joyful, because we know that suffering produces perseverance; perseverance, character; and character, hope. (Romans 5:3-4) I choose to rejoice always and focus my eyes on your promise and salvation, I am willing to follow the leading of the Holy Spirit, willing to change and rest in You, so that I may receive your good will and blessings when time have reached their fulfillment. (Ephesians 1:9-10)

Lord Jesus! I'm justified by my faith and I reject all of the accusations, worries, concerns, legalism, controls, condemnation, insecurity, excessive analyses of commentary, complex, chaotic, confusion, jealousy, I choose to listen, accept, and desire Your path that allows me to walk in freedom. (Psalm 119: 44-45)

I receive peace and joy from you, and I will rest in you, believing the guidance of the Holy Spirit. Unceasingly seeking the Lord in everything by prayer and supplication, with thanksgiving and follow Your guidance to go forth according to Your way. Please help me to keep a pure and clean heart, a steadfast spirit, and follow you whole heartedly. I will approach the throne of grace with confidence, so that I may receive mercy and find grace to help me in my time of need. (Hebrew 4:16), because there is joy of contentment before you and eternal blessings at Your right hand. Now, as we ask, we shall receive, therefore I will seek You for everything that I need, because even before I ask, You knew all my needs, and You will make my joy complete. (John 16:24)

For the Lord, my God, who takes hold of my right hand and says to me: "Do not fear; I will help you. (Isaiah 41:13) "God has held us since we were conceived, and have carried me since my birth. Even to my old age and gray hairs, God will sustain me. God has made me and He will carry me; He will sustain me and He will rescue me. (Isaiah 46:3-4)

Lord Jesus! Please help me not to sin when I am angry, and let me not hold anger until the sun goes down. (Ephesians 4:26). Make it so the enemy cannot take any foothold to steal my joy. Thank You for You are the center of my joy, You are the source of my strength. You are my all in all. I believe you will right the wrong for me, and Instead of my shame I will receive a double portion, and instead of disgrace I will rejoice in my inheritance. And so I will inherit a double portion in my land, and everlasting joy will be ours. For You, the LORD, love justice; You hate robbery and iniquity. In Your faithfulness You will reward me and make an everlasting covenant with me. (Isaiah 61:7-8)

Lord Jesus! Please help me to forgive others quickly, and not count their sins, with my will I chose to obey your command, I choose to forgive and choose to love, I also chose to forgive myself, for it is by grace I have been saved, through faith—and this not from myself, it is the gift of God. (Ephesians 2:8) Lord, thank you for forgiving my sins, iniquities and transgressions, because of your grace You forgave me, and I will also forgive those who hurt me, so that your grace and joy can overflow in my life. Because you loved me first, I also choose to love the people around me, including those who are not lovable. I rid myself of all moral filth and the evil that is prevalent, and humbly accept the

115

word planted in me, which can save me. (James 1:21)

Lord! Please help me understand your goodness and blame you no more, nor be angry at you. I know a lot of things that happened in my life is the work of the enemy, who comes to steal, kill and destroy. Lord of Compassion! I choose to believe in the blessings and grace you have for me; I reject all of the lies and deceptions and also ask you to forgive me for complaining to you when I did not know you.

Father God! I come before your throne of grace, commanding that everything that makes me depressed, worried, and bitter to go, I choose to believe in your good will, I choose to believe that every day of my life is the day the Lord has made and I will rejoice and be glad in it. (Psalm 118:24) By the strength given from Christ, I am able to rejoice under any circumstances. Abba Father! Please help me to be able to receive Your joy in my marriage, family, work, school, ministry, relationships, self-growth and all sorts of situations, a joy that is beyond human understanding. Help me to be able to face all of the situations in life, so I know what it is to be in need and I know what it is to have plenty. Help me learn the secret of being content in any and every situation, whether well fed or hungry, whether living in plenty or in want. So I can proclaim your joy, peace, and blessings of complaining, sighing and murmuring. Holy Spirit please come and fill me,

116

let me be filled with the joy and blessings of God.

Lord Jesus! You have set me above my companions by anointing me with the oil of joy (Hebrews 1:9). You give me the garment of praise to replace all spirits of heaviness. You replace in me beauty for ashes!

[Praise Proclamation]

(2 Chronicle 20:21-23 King Jehoshaphat appointed those who should sing to the LORD, and who should praise the beauty of holiness, as they went out before the army and were saying: "Praise the LORD, for His mercy *endures* forever." 22 Now when they began to sing and to praise, the LORD set ambushes against the people of Ammon, Moab, and Mount Seir, who had come against Judah; and they were defeated. "Faith is the substance of things hoped for, the evidence of things not seen. When we praise the Father, Son and Holy Spirit, give thanks for their goodness and mercy, we use the word of praise to proclaim the power of almighty God that reign in our life, and to replace negative emotions and cast out bondages of enemy, for example peace replace, insecurity, anxiety, nervousness, fear; light instead of darkness; joy v grief, sadness; freedom v bondage; lightening up v heavy yoke, self-acceptance v low self-esteem. When the Lord is enthroned in our life, enemies scatter and flee!! Hallelujah! Praise the Lord God, almighty, the creator of all things!)

✿ God is the Creator

✟ You alone are the LORD; I praise You! You have made heaven, The heaven of heavens, with all their host, The earth and everything on it, The seas and all that is in them, And You preserve them all. The host of heaven worships You. (Nehemiah 9:6)

✟ Oh Lord God! Creator of universe, maker of heavens and earth, and the world and everything in it! I praise You, I will stand every morning and evening to thank and praise You! (1 Chronicle 23:30)

✟ You are worthy, O Lord! To receive glory and honor and power; For You created all things, the whole earth shall praise You, And by Your will they exist and were created." (Rev. 4:11)! I praise You, You are the Lord of all earth! Creator of the universe and all things in it!

✟ I will open my mouth wide to praise You! You are the God of glory, creator of heaven and earth. You are worthy to be praised, Oh Lord!

✡ **God is Holy**

✟ Holy! Holy! Holy! Lord God Almighty, Who was and is and is to come!"

✟ "Holy, holy, holy is the LORD of hosts; The whole earth is full of Your glory!" (Isaiah 6:3)

✟ Dear heavenly Father! I want to walk with You, to have one heart, one mind with You. I want to give thanks to You for all things, praise You always! I will meditate

Your mercy, grace, kindness and Your wondrous work and glory! I will always praise, dance in front of You, let my spirit bubble before Your throne to honor Your holy name. For the Kingdom, honor and power, blessing and adoration, and all glory belongs to You alone!

✝ Jesus Christ! "Worthy is the Lamb who was slain, To receive power and riches and wisdom, and strength and honor and glory and blessing!" [13] And every creature which is in heaven and on the earth and under the earth and such as are in the sea, and all that are in them, I heard saying: "Blessing and honor and glory and power Be to Him who sits on the throne, And to the Lamb, forever and ever!" (Rev. 5:12-13)

✝ Be exalted, O LORD, in Your own strength! We will sing and praise Your power. (Psalm 21:13)

✝ "Blessed are You, LORD God of Israel, our Father, forever and ever.Yours, O LORD, *is* the greatness, The power and the glory, The victory and the majesty; For all *that is* in heaven and in earth is Yours; Yours *is* the kingdom, O LORD, And You are exalted as head over all.

[12] Both riches and honor *come* from You, And You reign over all. In Your hand is power and might; In Your hand it is to make great and to give strength to all.

[13] "Now therefore, our God, We thank You and praise Your glorious name.

✟ "We give You thanks, O Lord God Almighty, The One who is and who was and who is to come, because You have taken Your great power and reigned. (Rev.11:17)

✟ [1] Praise the LORD!
Praise God in Your sanctuary;
Praise Him in Your mighty firmament!

[2] Praise Him for Your mighty acts;
Praise You according to Your excellent greatness!

[3] Praise You with the sound of the trumpet;
Praise You with the lute and harp!

[4] Praise You with the timbrel and dance;
Praise You with stringed instruments and flutes!

[5] Praise You with loud cymbals;
Praise You with clashing cymbals!

[6] Let everything that has breath praise the LORD. Praise the LORD!

✿ God is God of all earth

✟ [5] Oh Lord God—I praise You, and worship You.

For my Maker *is* my husband, The LORD of hosts
is His name; And my Redeemer is the Holy One
of Israel; He is called the God of the whole earth.
(Isaiah 54:5)

✞ The heavens declare the glory of God;
And the firmament shows His handiwork.

² Day unto day utters speech,
And night unto night reveals knowledge.

³ There is no speech nor language
Where their voice is not heard.

⁴ Their line has gone out through all the earth,
And their words to the end of the world. (Psalm 19:1-
4)

✞ "Stand up and bless the LORD your God Forever
and ever!
"Blessed be Your glorious name,
Which is exalted above all blessing and praise!
⁶ You alone *are* the LORD;
You have made heaven,
The heaven of heavens, with all their host,
The earth and everything on it,
The seas and all that is in them,
And You preserve them all.
The host of heaven worships You.

(Nehemiah 9:5-6)

✡ The Lord God is the only True God

✞ Oh Lord! I praise You, You are the LORD, and *there is* no other; There is no God besides you.

✞   Therefore You are great, O Lord GOD. For *there is* none like You, nor is there any God besides You, according to all that we have heard with our ears. (2 Samuel 7:22)

✡ God is the King of all kings

✞ Oh God! My Lord! I praise You! All glory, honor, and praises and blessing be unto You! *You are* the blessed and only Potentate, the King of kings and Lord of lords, [16]who alone has immortality, dwelling in unapproachable light, whom no man has seen or can see, to whom be honor and everlasting power. Amen.(1 Timothy 6:15-16)

✞ Lord Jesus! I praise You, You humbled Yourself and became obedient to *the point of* death, even the death of the cross. [9]Therefore God also has highly exalted You and given You the name which is above every name, [10]that at the name of Jesus every knee should bow, of those in heaven, and of those on earth, and of those under the earth, [11]and *that* every

123

tongue should confess that Jesus Christ *is* Lord, to the glory of God the Father. (Philippians 2:9-12)

✝ Lord Jesus! I praise You! Father God raised You from the dead and seated *You* at His right hand in the heavenly places, [21]far above all principality and power and might and dominion, and every name that is named, not only in this age but also in that which is to come. [22]And He put all *things* under Your feet, and gave You *to be* head over all *things* to the church, [23]which is Your body, the fullness of You who fills all in all. (Ephesians 1:20-23)

✝ Oh Lord God! Praise You, You are the Ancient of Days, Your name is called Wonderful, Counselor, Mighty God, Everlasting Father, You live forever! (Daniel 7:9, Isaiah 9:6)

✝ Abba Father! I praise You, You are God our Savior, Who alone is wise, Be glory and majesty, Dominion and power, Both now and forever. Amen. (Jude 25)

✡ God is Love

✝ Oh Lord! I praise You, You are God of love, You are love! (1 John 4:16)

✝ Oh Lord! I praise You! You in Your mercy have led

forth

The people whom You have redeemed;

You have guided us in Your strength

To Your holy habitation. You are my praise, and You are my God, who has done for me these great and awesome things which my eyes have seen. (Exodus 15:13, Due. 10:21)

✟ I will praise You, O Lord, among the peoples;

I will sing to You among the nations.

[10]For Your mercy reaches unto the heavens,

And Your truth unto the clouds.

[11]Be exalted, O God, above the heavens;

Let Your glory be above all the earth.

(Psalm 57:9-11)

✟ Oh Lord God! I will sing of Your power;

Yes, I will sing aloud of Your mercy in the morning;

For You have been my defense

And refuge in the day of my trouble.

(Psalm 59:16)

✟ Oh Lord! Because Your loving kindness is better than life,

My lips shall praise You.

✟ How precious *is* Your loving kindness, O God!

Therefore the children of men put their trust under the shadow of Your wings. (Psalm 36:7)

✞ I will worship toward Your holy temple,
And praise Your name
For Your loving kindness and Your truth;
For You have magnified Your word above all Your
name. (Psalm 138:2)

✞ Oh Lord! I offer You a sacrifice of praise! For You
have made me most blessed forever;
You have made me exceedingly glad with Your
presence. (Psalm 21:6)

✞ ¹I will bless the LORD at all times;
His praise *shall* continually be in my mouth.
²My soul shall make its boast in the LORD;
The humble shall hear of it and be glad.
³ Oh, magnify the LORD with me,
And let us exalt His name together.
(Psalm 34:1-3)

✞ Blessed be the God and Father of our Lord Jesus
Christ, the Father of mercies and God of all comfort,
(2 Corinthian 1:3)

✡ God Is Light

✞ The LORD is my light and my salvation;
Whom shall I fear? I praise You!
The LORD is the strength of my life;
Of whom shall I be afraid? (Psalm 27:1)

✟ Oh God! I praise You! For with You is the fountain of life;
In Your light we see light. (Psalm36:9)

✟ Oh Lord! I praise You!when I hope on You, my soul lifts up, no more cast down, You are the light , the help of my countenance and my God. (Psalm 42:11)

✟ Oh God, I praise You that You send out Your light and Your truth!
Let them lead me;
Let them bring me to Your holy hill
And to Your tabernacle.
[4]Then I will go to the altar of God,
To God my exceeding joy;
And on the harp I will praise You,
O God, my God. (Psalm 43:3-4)

✡ God's Glory

✟ Father God! I want to Declare Your glory among the nations,
Your wonders among all peoples.
Give to the LORD, O families of the peoples,
Give to the LORD glory and strength.
(1Chronicle 16:24,28)

✟ Be exalted, O God, above the heavens;
Let Your glory *be* above all the earth.

(Psalm 57:5)

✝ In God is my salvation and my glory;
The rock of my strength,
And my refuge, is in God. (Psalm 62:7)

✝ Oh Lord God! I will sing out the honor of Your
name;
Make Your praise glorious. (Psalm 66:2)

✝ Oh Lord! Blessed be Your glorious name forever!
And let the whole earth be filled *with* Your glory.
Amen and Amen. (Psalm 72:19)

✝ All nations whom You have made
Shall come and worship before You, O Lord,
And shall glorify Your name.
I will praise You, O Lord my God, with all my heart,
And I will glorify Your name forevermore.
(Psalm 86:9,12)

✝ So the nations shall fear the name of the LORD,
And all the kings of the earth Your glory.
 (Psalm 102:15)

✝ The LORD *is* high above all nations,
His glory above the heavens. I praise You!
(Psalm 113:4)

128

✞ Yes, they shall sing of the ways of the LORD,
For great *is* the glory of the LORD. (Psalm 138:5)

✞ Let them praise the name of the LORD,
For His name alone is exalted;
His glory *is* above the earth and heaven.
(Psalm 148:13)

✞ Oh Lord! We Praise You! All people glorify the
LORD in the dawning light, The name of the LORD
God of Israel in the coastlands of the sea. Let them
give glory to the LORD, and declare His praise in
the coastlands. (Isaiah 24:15, 42:12)

✡ God is Faithful

✞ O Lord! I praise You! Your mercy, O LORD, is in
the heavens;
Your faithfulness reaches to the clouds.
(Psalm 36:5)

✞ I will sing of the mercies of the LORD forever, With
my mouth will I make known Your faithfulness to all
generations.
[2]For I have said, "Mercy shall be built up forever;Your
faithfulness You shall establish in the very heavens."
[5] And the heavens will praise Your wonders, O LORD;
Your faithfulness also in the assembly of the saints.
[6] For who in the heavens can be compared to the

LORD?

Who among the sons of the mighty can be likened to the LORD?

[8] O LORD God of hosts,

Who is mighty like You, O LORD?

Your faithfulness also surrounds You.

(Psalm 89:1-8)

✞ Heavenly Father, the LORD my God, You are God, the faithful God who keeps covenant and mercy for a thousand generations with those who love You and keep Your commandments;

✡ God is Just

✞ Oh Lord! I praise You! You Yourself are righteous and that You justify and accept as righteous those who has [true] faith in Jesus. (Roman 3:26)

✞ Oh Lord! I praise You! I give all glory to You, for the hour of Your judgment has come; and all nation and all people, every tongue worship You who made heaven and earth, the sea and springs of water." (Rev. 14:7)

✞ Oh Lord! I will praise the LORD according to His righteousness,

And I will sing praise to the name of the LORD Most High. (Psalm 7:17)

✞ Oh Lord! I praise You! We rejoice in the LORD! Praise You that You have kept our heart upright, We will praise the LORD with the harp; Make melody to You with an instrument of ten strings. [3]Sing to You a new song; Play skillfully with a shout of joy. (Psalm 33:1-3)

✡ God Is Mercy

✞ Father God! I praise You for You are God, gracious and merciful. I praise You for Your great mercy!

✞ Father God! I praise You for You are merciful and gracious, and You are compassionate. Thank You for cleansing me daily with the precious blood of Jesus Christ, Your word and power of the Holy Spirit, and You make me partaker of Your divine nature, so that I can inherit Your abundance and glorify Your name! (2 Peter 1:4)

✞ Oh Lord! I praise You and thank You, You are a God full of mercy and grace, A bruised reed You will not break,
And smoking flax You will not quench, thank You for releasing me from heavy burden, You have mercy on me, understand my weaknesses, pain and accept me as who I am. Father God! I give You praise! You are my strength, help, my rock, You make me strong when I am weak, make me rich when I am poor, blind

can see, You overturned my life, gave me miracle break through, whenever I am weak I can be strong in You. May all the glory, honor be to You, God almighty!

✢ Father God! I praise You! You are God, Ready to pardon, Gracious and merciful, Slow to anger, Abundant in kindness. (Nehemiah 9:17) Bless the LORD, O my soul; And all that is within me, bless Your holy name!
²Bless the LORD, O my soul,
And forget not all Your benefits:
³ You forgive all my iniquities,
and heal all my diseases,
⁴ You redeem my life from destruction,
and crown me with loving kindness and tender mercies
(Psalm 103:1-4)

✡ <u>Wonder Working God</u>

✢ Oh Lord—I praise You! You are the God who does wonders; You have declared Your strength among the peoples. (Psalm 77:14)

✢ "Who is like You, O LORD, among the gods?
Who *is* like You, glorious in holiness,
Fearful in praises, doing wonders?
(Exodus 15:11)

✢ Oh Lord—I praise You! You do great things past

finding out,

Yes, wonders without number. (Job 9:10)

✝ Blessed *be* the LORD God, the God of Israel,

Who only does wondrous things! (Psalm 72:18)

✝ Oh Lord! You *are* the God who does wonders;

You have declared Your strength among the peoples.

(Psalm 77:14)

✝ Father God! I praise you! For You are the Lord

who heals me. (Exodus 15:26)

✝ Oh Lord—I praise You, You sent Your word and

healed us,

And delivered us from our destructions.

(Psalm 107:20)

✝ Oh Lord! I praise you! When I Trust in the

LORD with all our heart, and lean not on our own

understanding;

^{6} In all our ways acknowledge You,

And You shall direct our paths.

^{7} When we are not be wise in our own eyes;

Fear the LORD and depart from evil.

AS we honor the LORD with our possessions,

And with the first fruits of all our increase;

You will heal our flesh and strengthen our bones, and

our barns will be filled with plenty,

And our vats will overflow with new wine.
(Prov. 3:1-10)

✟ Lord Jesus, I praise you! For You are wounded
for our transgressions, You were bruised for our
iniquities;
The chastisement for our peace was upon You,
And by Your stripes we are healed. (Isaiah 53:5)

✟ Oh Lord! Praise You! For You heal me, O LORD,
and I shall be healed; Praise you for You save me, and
I shall be saved,
For You are my praise. (Jeremiah 17:14)

✟ Oh Lord! I Praise You! For to us who fear Your
name
The Sun of Righteousness shall arise, We praise
You for You hide us under Your wings and there are
healing in Your wings; and You make us go out and
grow fat like stall-fed calves!
(Malachi 4:2)

✟   Oh Lord! I praise you, for You are Jehovah
Jireh — My Supplier.
You are able to make all grace abound toward us,
that we, always having all sufficiency in all things,
may have an abundance for every good work. (2
Corinthian 9:8)

✡ God Gives

✝ Father God! May all the glory, honor and praises be unto You, For You are a generous God, You even gave Your only begotten Son to us. (John 3:16)

✝ Oh Lord! My God, I praise You, that You test the heart and have pleasure in uprightness. As for me, in the uprightness of my heart I have willingly offered all these things [18]O LORD God, keep this forever in the intent of the thoughts of the heart of Your people, and fix our heart toward You. and give my offspring a loyal heart to keep Your commandments and Your testimonies and Your statutes, to do all these things, and to complete works that pleases Your heart. (1 Chronicle 29:17-19)

✡ God Hears Prayer

✝ Father God! I give You all praises and honor, for before I call, You will answer; and while I am still speaking, You will hear me. (Isaiah 65:24)

✝ Father God! I praise You, thank You for helping me to grow in the grace and knowledge of our Lord and Savior Jesus Christ. To You be the glory both now and forever. Amen. (2 Peter 3:18)

✝ Oh Lord! My God! I sing praise songs to You!

135

Then I will go to the altar of God,
To God my exceeding joy;
And on the harp I will praise You, O God, my God
We will sing praises to God, sing praises!
Sing praises to our King, sing praises. For You are
the King of all the earth; We will sing praises with
understanding! (Psalm 43:4; 47:6-7)

✠ Oh God! I bless Your Holy name, I praise You. For
You are Jehovah Roi- my shepherd; You look after me,
You lead me in the paths of righteousness for Your
name's sake. (Psalm 23:1-3)

✡ God is My Banner of Victory

✠ Oh Lord God! I give You all the praises, For You
are Jehovah Nissi- my Banner, My victory, You
always lead us in triumph in Christ.
 (2 Corinthian 2:14)

✠ Oh Lord God! Who is like You, among all gods?!
Who is like You, glorious in holiness, Fearful in
praises, doing wonders? "Your right hand, O LORD,
has become glorious in power; Your right hand, O
LORD, has dashed the enemy in pieces. And in the
greatness of Your excellence, You have overthrown
those who rose against You; You sent forth Your
wrath; It consumed them like stubble. (Exodus 15:2-19)

136

✞ Oh Lord! I will praise You with all my heart, for You are Jehovah Shalom- my peace, You are the God of peace Who will crush Satan under my feet shortly. (Roman 16:20)

✞ Oh Lord! I praise You, for You are the God Who vindicated me. I praise You for Your loving kindness are always with me. Thank You for You Redeemed me and be merciful to me. My foot stands in an even place; In the congregations I will bless the LORD. (Psalm 26)

✞ Oh God! I praise you! You are my help and my deliverer; O LORD. (Psalm 70:5)

✞ Oh Lord! I give You praise! Out of the mouth of babes and nursing infants You have ordained strength,
Because of Your enemies,
That You may silence the enemy and the avenger. (Psalm 8:2)

✞   In God (I will praise Your word),
In the LORD (I will praise Your word),
In God I have put my trust;
I will not be afraid.
What can man do to me? (Psalm 56:10-11)

✞ Oh Lord! I praise You, For You have delivered

my soul from death.Have You not *kept* my feet from falling,
That I may walk before God
In the light of the living? (Psalm 56:13)

✿ <u>God is My Rock</u>

✟ In God *is* my salvation and my glory;
The rock of my strength, *And* my refuge, *is* in God.
(Psalm 62:7)

✟ "My heart rejoices in the LORD;
My horn is exalted in the LORD.
I smile at my enemies,
Because I rejoice in Your salvation.
[2] "No one is holy like the LORD,
For *there is* none besides You,
Nor *is there* any rock like our God.
(1 Samuel 2:2)

✟ "The LORD *is* my rock and my fortress and my deliverer;
The God of my strength, in whom I will trust;
My shield and the horn of my salvation,
My stronghold and my refuge;
My Savior, You save me from violence. (2 Samuel 22:4)

✟ Oh Lord' I will wait for You, O You my Strength;
For God *is* my defense.

My God of mercy shall come to meet me;
God shall let me see *my desire* on my enemies.(Psalm
59:9-10)

✠ God is my Strength

✞ I will love You, O LORD, my strength. I praise You
(Psalm 18:1)

✞ The LORD *is* my strength and song,
And You have become my salvation;
You are my God, and I will praise You;
My father's God, and I will exalt You.
(Exodus 15:2)

✞ The LORD *is* my strength and my shield;
My heart trusted in You, and I am helped;
Therefore my heart greatly rejoices,
And with my song I will praise You. (Psalm 28:7)

✞ Oh Lord! I will wait for You, O You my Strength;
For God *is* my defense.
To You, O my Strength, I will sing praises;
For God *is* my defense,
 My God of mercy. (Psalm 59:9,17)

✞ [2] Behold, God *is* my salvation,
I will trust and not be afraid;
For YAH, the LORD, *is* my strength and song;

You also has become my salvation.' (Isaiah 12:2)

✟ Oh LORD, I praise You, For You
Who formed Me from the womb *to be* Your Servant,
To bring Jacob back to You,
So that Israel is gathered to You
For I shall be glorious in the eyes of the LORD,
 And My God shall be My strength. (Isaiah 49:5)

✟ Oh LORD! I praise You for You are my strength;
You will make my feet like deer's feet,
And You will make me walk on my high hills.
(Habakkuk 3:19)

✡ <u>God is My Shield</u>

✟ Father God! I praise You! For You, O LORD, *are* a
shield for me,
My glory and the One who lifts up my head. (Psalm
3:3)

✟ Oh Lord! I praise You! You will guard the feet of
Your saints,
But the wicked shall be silent in darkness. (1 Samuel
2:9)

✟ Oh Lord! I praise You! You hide me under Your
wings and in the cleaves of rock, You redeemed us
and made us received Your everlasting salvation,

blessed by Your riches grace. I praise You!
You make me to lie down in green pastures;
You lead me beside the still waters. You restore my
soul;
Praise You, For You prepare a table before me in
the presence of my enemies;
You anoint my head with oil;
My cup runs over. Surely goodness and mercy shall
follow me
All the days of my life; (Psalm 23:1-6) Father God,
You are worth to be praised and blessed.

✞ The God of my strength, in whom I will trust;
My shield and the horn of my salvation,
My stronghold and my refuge;
My Savior, You save me from violence. (2 Samuel
22:3)

✞   The LORD is my rock and my fortress and my
deliverer;
My God, my strength, in whom I will trust;
My shield and the horn of my salvation, my
stronghold.
I praise You! (Psalm 18:2)

✞   The LORD *is* my strength and my shield;
My heart trusted in You, and I am helped;
Therefore my heart greatly rejoices,
And with my song I will praise You. (Psalm 28:7)

✞ You *are* my hiding place and my shield;
I hope in Your word. (Psalm 119:114)

✞ Oh Lord! I praise You, You are my loving kindness
and my fortress,
My high tower and my deliverer,
My shield and *the One* in whom I take refuge,
Who subdues my people under me. (Psalm 144:2)

[Prayer for Rejoicing in My Job]

[Giving my Job as an offering to God]

Father God! I offer my job to You, I ask You to reign in my job. I thank You for the wonderful "job" You have provided me now. I put all my trust in You, believing that my present job is what You have provided me for me to experience Your abundant grace to break all the enemy's yoke, and to become a overcomer, despite all my circumstances, no matter whether it's good or bad. I thank You for my boss, my colleagues and all my working experiences. I thank You that You use this job experience to train and mold me, so that I become worthy to receive my calling and complete it. I can also do all things through Christ who strengthens me. (Philippians 4:13)

In Jesus' name I declare: I believe firmly that You, Father God, have arranged the most suitable job for me through every step of my learning process and life experiences, I believe that You make all things work together for my good. I pray that You will grant me all the power, wisdom and abilities according to my job requirements. I want to experience Your faithfulness, love and glory in my job. I renounce all the enemy's lies and all wrong attitude about wandering and orphan spirit, I reject all the negative thoughts that I am not or inadequate for this job. Oh

143

Lord! This is the job You gave to me that no one can replace. The Scripture says: He who tills his land will be satisfied with bread, but he who follows frivolity *is* devoid of understanding. The hand of the diligent will rule, but the lazy *man* will be put to forced labor. (Proverb 12:11,24)

[Mold into Jesus' Likeness]

Oh Lord! Help me in whatever I do, do it heartily, as to the Lord and not to men, [24] knowing that from the Lord I will receive the reward of the inheritance; for I serve the Lord Christ. (Colossians 3: 23-24) Oh Lord! Please help me also aspire to lead a quiet life, to mind my own business, and to work with my own hands, [12]that I may walk properly toward those who are outside, and *that* I may lack nothing. (1 Thessalonians 4:11-12) Lord please help me to keep my heart with all diligence, for out of it *spring* the issues of life. Put away from me a deceitful mouth, and put perverse lips far from me. Let my eyes look straight ahead, and my eyelids look right before me. Ponder the path of my feet, and let all my ways be established. Do not turn to the right or the left; Remove my foot from evil. (Proverb 4:23-27) That I walk not in the counsel of the ungodly, nor stands in the path of sinners, nor sits in the seat of the scornful; But my delight *is* in the law of the LORD, and in His law I meditates day and night, and I will be blessed. (Psalm 1:1-2)

Lord, please help me to keep a upright heart, good virtue, give me strength to reject all the temptations from the enemy, that I may be partakers of the divine nature, having escaped the corruption that is in the world through lust.(2 Peter 1:1-4). Lord, please help me have no greed, no jealousy, no bribing, with all lowliness and gentleness, with longsuffering, bearing with one another in love, endeavoring to keep the unity of the Spirit in the bond of peace. (Ephesians 4:2-3) but, speaking the truth in love, so we may grow up in all things into You who is the head—Christ—(Ephesians 4:15), let all the word in my mouth and my behavior glorify Your name and bless others, help me to judge all things according to Your way and the heart of Christ, not turn left or right, not lust over reputations or fame and profit that does not belong to me. Lord, Please lead me in the path of God's will, Jesus' likeness and fruit of Holy Spirit (love, joy, peace, longsuffering, kindness, goodness, faithfulness, gentleness, and self-control)to be the guidance of my work, that I can testify Your glorious presence and blessing on my job.

Lord! Help me to know how to appreciate those who have helped me, to applause other's strength, tolerate their short comings, understand their weaknesses, but in lowliness of mind that I esteem others better than myself, and look out not only for my own interests, but also for the interests of others.(Philippians 2:3-4), to love my neighbors, care of group benefit, enjoy to cooperate with others, make peace with others like blending salt, bring comfort, encouragement and edifying, blessing words with a humble heart, to arise and shine for You in my job environment.

[Declare God's Promise]

In Jesus' name, I declare: The Lord God make_____
multiply and fruitful, make _____ stronger then my
enemies. (Psalm 105:24) The Lord God is _____'s
living God, Blessed *be* _____'s Rock! Let the God
of _____'s salvation be exalted. Praise you that
You led ____'s path, lighten the darkness before
_____'s eye, You made _____ run through
a troop: by You my God have I leaped over a wall. I
praise You, Oh God! *As for* You, Your way *is* perfect;
The word of the LORD *is* proven; You are a shield to
all who trust in You. For You have armed _____
with strength for the battle; You make _____'s
way perfect, You makes _____'s feet like the *feet*
of deer, And sets _____ on _____'s high places.
You teach _____'s hands to make war, so that
_____'s arms can bend a bow of bronze. Father
God, "You have also given _____ the shield of Your
salvation; Your right hand has held _____ up,
Your gentleness has made _____ great. You
enlarged _____'s path under _____, so
_____'s feet did not slip. They have fallen under
_____'s feet. For You have armed _____ with
strength for the battle; You have subdued under
_____those who rose up against _____. You
have also given _____ the necks of _____'s
enemies, so that _____destroyed those who hated
_____. (Psalm 18: 28-40) Oh Lord! I praise You,

147

You are the LORD who lives! Blessed *be* my Rock!
Let the God of _____'s salvation be exalted. Oh
Lord! Let Your name be exalted among all nations, by
Your riches glory and great abundant blessings, may
You draw all men back to You, and know You, trust
You, experience You!

[Be Good Stewards]

Oh Lord! Please teach me to be Your good steward,
to have wisdom, principals that came from You to
manage my finance and money, so that I will not fall
into the financial trap and foothold, I will follow You
always , and not turn to worship mammon (Exodus
20:5), far away from covetous and stealing other's
properties (Ephesians 4:28) (including using pirate
copy (when I can afford original), (taking small
advantage of others), fornication and abundance of
luxury (Rev. 18:3-8), gaining without laboring, exploit
wage earners, oppresses the poor to increase riches,
bribe (Proverb 22:16), laziness (Proverb 10:4), stingy,
Selfishness...etc. all the ungodly wrong mind set of
financial management, keep my heart to have mercy
to those poor neighbors, love to scatter (Proverb 11:24),
faithfully giving tithes (Luke 6:38), sows bountifully
also reap bountifully. (2 Corinthians 9:6), I will use
where the Lord direct me to use, the Lord make me
abundant to use in the Kingdom of God to bless many
to hear the good news of salvation, to know God, to

testify God's love, glory and abounding grace.

[Enlarge Territory]

Lord Jesus! Please lift Your servant up in the market place, for Your name sake. Please help me to focus my goal on Your ways, help me to depart away from the counsel of the ungodly, only to focus on You. Help me to be attentive when I work, give me wisdom, knowledge, abilities of being observant, experiences and good virtous character. Please release Your revelations, visions, strategies of development, clear goals, enlarge my territory, lift up my eye sight. Lord! Please help me to keep upright attitude, continuously to have new ideas and break through, and welcoming all new challenges and changes, give me wisdom to see and resolve problems, help me to keep optimistic mind and responsible attitude, reveal high efficiency and good quality performance, so that I shall be the head not be the tail, and I shall be above only, and not be beneath. Please give me supernatural chances and resources, that I can supernaturally turn around, have miracle break through, supernatural promotion and increase, to make possible from impossible, rules and regulations and laws will be edited for our benefit, so that we will receive good reputation for the Lord's name sake.

Lord, I pray that You rise up more of Your servants

in every industry of the market place, no matter is workers, office staff, supervisor, manager, executive officers, CEO, make us carry the vision of "Transforming market place for Jesus" with us to go forward. Make us be the light and salt in our industry, to spread good news, testify the name of Jesus Christ, minister to God's people as our calling. Lord, make us to be influential in our atmosphere, evangelize Your name, transform our department, school, industry, nation, to lift Your name on high, glorify Your name in market place.

[Preface for Appendix Prayer User]

Q1. After conversion to be a Christian does not mean we have no more sin to deal with. The definition of "sin" has to be defined by God and from the principle of Bible. "Sin" includes:

◆ Sin: Rebel, adversary, and transgression of divine law: the sin of Adam that comes from generational line.

✟ Exodus 34:7 keeping mercy for thousands, forgiving iniquity and transgression and sin, by no means clearing *the guilty,* visiting the iniquity of the fathers upon the children and the children's children to the third and the fourth generation." As a Christian, Jesus became curse for us on the cross, so that we can enter into blessing. But most of us we did not apply the authority that the Lord bestowed on us to break the right of generational iniquities.

✟ Psalm 51:5 Behold, I was brought forth in iniquity, and in sin my mother conceived me.

✟ Romans 5:12 Therefore, just as through one man sin entered the world, and death through sin, and thus death spread to all men, because all sinned—

✟ Romans 5:19 For as by one man's disobedience many were made sinners, so also by one Man's obedience many will be made righteous. (Disobedience to God's will, or turn away from God is sin.)

How to deal with it: Use prayers of appendix 1 prayer for generational iniquity, prayer of confessing transgressions of family line ... to break curses in Deuteronomy 28. (Daniel 9:5, 8, Nehemiah 9:2, 16)

◆ Iniquity: Do things against God's law, lack of justice or righteousness; wickedness; injustice, 2. A wicked act; sin

✝ Leviticus 5:1 IF ANYONE sins in that he is sworn to testify and has knowledge of the matter, either by seeing or hearing of it, but fails to report it, then he shall bear his iniquity and willfulness.

✝ Leviticus 5:17 If anyone sins and does any of the things the Lord has forbidden, though he was not aware of it, yet he is guilty and shall bear his iniquity.

✿ How to deal with iniquities:

✝ Ask the Holy Spirit to convict, then confess/repent for own sins in thought, word, behavior and any deeds that hurt others, ask for forgiveness from God, and ask the Lord to heal all the insecurity, uneasiness, sickness, insomnia...etc.

✝ Ask God to give you faith and ability to sin no more. Also, ask for courage and chances to ask forgiveness from the person you hurt. Bless the person who has been hurt by you.

✝ Declare the Lord's salvation in Jesus' name.

✝ Use "Cleansing prayer" to cut all ungodly spirit, soul, body linking, sever all ungodly linkings between you and those people that the Holy Spirit have revealed to you. Arrest and bind the evil spirits related to the sin, cast them out from you and then break all curses. (Note: Must be spoken out!)

✝ Please also refer to the prayer related to sexual sin, abortion and free from inner vow in appendix 1.

◆ Transgressions: Violation of a law, command, etc.; sin.

✝ Exodus 23:21 Give heed to Him, listen to and obey His voice; be not rebellious before Him or provoke Him, for He will not pardon your transgression;

✝ All ways of dealing with sin must follow God's way.

✝ 1 John 1:9 If we [freely] admit that we have sinned and confess our sins, He is faithful and just (true to His own nature and promises) and will forgive our sins

153

[dismiss our lawlessness] and [continuously] cleanse us from all unrighteousness [everything not in conformity to His will in purpose, thought, and action].

✝ Matthew 6:14-15 For if you forgive people their trespasses [their reckless and willful sins, leaving them, letting them go, and giving up resentment], your heavenly Father will also forgive you.

✝ Therefore, we need to forgive our ancestors for the bondages they have caused us, and any influences that have affected us due to their sin. Lord Jesus has already completed all the redemptive work on the cross, we now need to use our free will to choose and believe Him, follow Him and agree with Him. Also, utilize the authority He has given us to cast out evil spirit, and heal the sick, raise the dead and set the captive free.

◆ **Dealing Method: Same as dealing with iniquities.**

Q2: Right Altitude for Christians during Ancestral worship ritual.

✝ Worship only your God, the true God.

✝ Do not offer any thing to idols, ancestor, dead (especially do not offer joss stick, water, flower to familial spirits in family line.), never bow or kneel or any form of worship.

✝ Ask the Lord to reign in our family. Intercede and bless everyone who is still under bondage or confusion, stand in the gap to confess and acknowledge the sins of the family line, ask for The Lord to have mercy and grace on them, to deliver them from the bondage of Chinese cultural traditional customs. (Colossians 2:8 Beware lest anyone cheat you through philosophy and empty deceit, according to the tradition of men, according to the basic principles of the world, and not according to Christ.) note: use silent prayer when interceding.

✝ Lift the name of the Lord high when the other family members go through the process of ancestral worship. (Praise or pray in silent mode or under your breath. Also you can pray in tongues quietly)

✝ Worship the Lord in truth, and not give glory to the other gods (including the blessing or protection from ancestors and dead people)

[Generational Iniquities]

Father God, I come before You in the name of Jesus Christ, My Savior and Lord. I confess that both my ancestors and I have sinned and done evil in Your sight.

Thank you, Father, for sending Your only Son, Jesus, to die in my place; to pay the penalty for my sins through His shed blood and to bear the punishment for the sins and iniquities of my ancestors on His bruised and broken body on the Cross. Thank You that He is my Holy Scapegoat. Thank you, Father, that by His wound I was healed.

I choose now to confess and renounce all the sins and iniquities of my ancestors back to the beginning of my family line all the way to Adam and Eve.

I confess any ungodly thoughts and negative emotions that have had an ill effect on my family line and on me. I confess the sins of unrighteousness, evil, maliciousness, deceit and treachery, rebellion, negative anger, rage, arrogance, bitterness, sarcasms, covetous greed, stealing, robbery, jealousy, domination and control, dictatorship, stubbornness, boasting, fear, hatred, manipulation, pride, competition, resentment, self-pity, shame, denial, pessimism, passiveness, fatality, nega-tive, doubt, impatience, cruelty, mercilessness, violence, murder, skepticism, hating God, secret backbiter, lovelessness, inventor of new evils, disobedience and undutiful to parent, hatred of women, despising of men in my family line.

I confess the operation of the sin of rejection in my family line, especially those which are affecting my marriage and my family—Rejection, abandonment, abuse, adoption, criticism, slander, death, betrayal, divorce/separation, emotional hardness, gossip, isolation, loneliness, accusation, torture, ungodly judgments, argument, over-protection, blame shift, perfectionism.

I confess any sin that has led to mental illness in my family line—anxiety, depression, phobias, obsessions, insane, manic depres-sion, and schizophrenia, multiple personality/ identity disorder.

I confess any sins of addictions in my family line— alcohol, nicotine, caffeine, food, anorexia, bulimia, drugs, opium, gambling, hoarding, shopping, television, games, exercise, sex, workaholic, stealing, and the use of tranquilizers or other type of comforter.

I confess sexual sins in my family line, known and unknown—abuse, adultery, fornication, polygamy, bestiality, orgy, homosexuality, incest, lust, masturbation, perversions, and pornography.

I confess any sin which led to the destruction of marriage through divorce in my family line.

I confess any sin that has led to untimely death in my family line—death of disappointment or resentment, still birth, early death, miscarriages, murder, suicide, terminations/abortions, death of accident, traumatic death. I confess any sin of unresolved grief from death.

I confess any lying and/or deception in my family line.

I confess any sin of false guilt and fear in my family line—false responsibility, fear of failure, fear of punishment, fear of man, fear of disapproval, fear of authority, fear of death, feelings of guilt, hiding, insecurity. I confess any feelings of needing to be punished or blamed—self-condemnation, lying and shame.

I confess the effects of war on my family—death, destruction, fear, hatred, murder, insecurity, nervousness, famine, separation, sickness, ill, poverty, tiredness, wandering, imprisonment, torturing, traumatic death, cruelty, violence, shedding innocent blood, strengthless, helpless, hopeless, sadness, grief, captivated, being surrounded, no rescuer, decomposed, no one burry the corps, corps being exposed to wild beast, trauma, accident, handicapped, disvalue human life, curse of the land.

I confess any sin of religious restrictions and constrictions, either from a Christian denomination or a church, or from different false religions or occult involvement in my family line—Ancestral worship, Dragon worship, Buddhism, Taoism, Confucianism, New age, Freemasonry, Jehovah Witnesses, Mormons, Muslim, saint worship, religious control and domination, legalism, oppression.

I confess any involvement and tampering with occult power, witchcraft or the hidden things of darkness. I understand any supernatural powers are sin if it is not come from God.

I confess any sins of pronouncements, inner vows, false judgments or curses in my family line.

I confess times where the fathers in my family line have not taught their children the ways of God. I confess where the mothers in my family line have dominated, manipulated, controlled and/or despised the men in my family line.

I confess and recognize possible ungodly attitudes and belief systems in my family line or cultural

159

background—competition, comparison, deception, distrust, envy/jealousy, failure, faultfinding, rejection, forgetfulness, frivolity, robbery, greed, laziness, lying, materialism, lustful of flesh, passiveness, blind obedience, performance, pessimism, poverty, in debt, tiredness, racism, suspicion, unworthiness, valueless, worry, self- sacrifice, behavior orientation.

I confess any sin which led to hereditary illnesses and/or weaknesses in my family line,(name every disease out loud).

Father God, I come before You in the name of Jesus, confessing and renouncing these sins in my family lines. I now lay the punishment, curses and inherited weaknesses on Jesus, my Scapegoat, on His bruised and broken body on the cross and release myself from their ill effects. Thank you, Lord, that I can cast my burdens on You, I receive my freedom.

By an act of my will, I unreservedly forgive my ancestors for their sins and release my ancestors into the freedom of my forgiveness. I will not blame them anymore.

I confess and renounce my own sins in these areas, especially as they affect my family. I repent and turn from them and ask You to forgive and cleanse me with the precious blood of Jesus. Thank you, Lord Jesus, for cleansing me.

Please heal me, renew me and lead me in Your way, Lord Jesus. Amen.

[Renunciation of Sins of My Family Line]
Roman 1: 18-32

[18] For the wrath of God is revealed from heaven against all ungodliness and unrighteousness of men, who suppress the truth in unrighteousness,

[Pray] I confess and repent of my family line for all the ungodliness and unrighteousness that suppressed and hindered the Truth by their wickedness.

[19-21] [19] because what may be known of God is manifest in them, for God has shown *it* to them. [20] For since the creation of the world His invisible *attributes* are clearly seen, being understood by the things that are made, *even* His eternal power and Godhead, so that they are without excuse, [21] because, although they knew God, they did not glorify *Him* as God, nor were thankful, but became futile in their thoughts, and their foolish hearts were darkened.

[Pray] I confess and repent for those who, although they knew God, they neither glorified Him as God nor gave thanks to Him because their thinking was futile and their foolish hearts were darkened.

22 Professing to be wise, they became fools, 23 and changed the glory of the incorruptible God into an image made like corruptible man—and birds and four-footed animals and creeping things.

[Pray] I repent for all those who became fools and exchanged the glory of the immortal God for images made to look like mortal man and birds and animals and reptiles.

24 Therefore God also gave them up to uncleanness, in the lusts of their hearts, to dishonor their bodies among themselves.

[Pray] I repent for the sinful desires of my ancestors' hearts who gave their hearts to sexual impurity for the degrading of their bodies with one another.

25 who exchanged the truth of God for the lie, and worshiped and served the creature rather than the Creator, who is blessed forever. Amen.

[Pray] I repent for all those who exchanged the truth of God for a lie, and worshipped and served created things rather than the Creator- who is forever praised.

26 For this reason God gave them up to vile passions.

For even their women exchanged the natural use for what is against nature.

[Pray] I repent for the shameful lusts of my ancestors and for the women who exchanged natural relations for unnatural ones.

[27] Likewise also the men, leaving the natural use of the woman, burned in their lust for one another, men with men committing what is shameful, and receiving in themselves the penalty of their error which was due.

[Pray] I repent for the men in my family line who abandoned natural relations with women and were inflamed with lust for one another, men who committed indecent acts with other men, and received in themselves the due penalty for their perversion.

[28]Furthermore, since they did not think it worthwhile to retain the knowledge of God, he gave them over to a depraved mind, to do what ought not to be done .

[Pray] I repent for those who did not think it worthwhile to retain the knowledge of God, and therefore they were turned over to a depraved mind, to do what ought not to be done.

[29]They have become filled with every kind of wickedness, evil, greed and depravity. They are full of

163

envy, murder, strife, deceit and malice.

[Pray] I repent for all those who have been filled with every kind of wickedness, evil, greed and depravity, and for all those who were full of envy, murder, strife, deceit and malice.

They are gossips, [30]slanderers, God-haters, insolent, arrogant and boastful; they invent ways of doing evil; they disobey their parents; [31]they are senseless, faithless, heartless, and ruthless.

[Pray] I repent for all those who were gossips, slanders, God-haters, insolent, arrogant and boastful; for all those who invented ways of doing evil, who were disobedient to their parents, who were senseless, faithless, heartless, and ruthless

[32]Although they know God's righteous decree that those who do such things deserve death, they not only continue to do these very things but also approve of those who practice them

[Pray] I repent for those who although they knew God's righteous decree that those who do such things deserve death, they not only continued to do these very things but also approved of those who practiced them.

(Revised from Paul L. Cox Ministry by Sozo Ministries Inc)

[Confess and Repent for the Sin of Ancestral Worship]

Dear Heavenly Father, I confess that my ancestors, my family members and I have followed the Chinese cultural traditions to worship the dead and ancestors during important festivals like new year, tomb sweeping day, moon festival or during marriage ceremonies and birthdays, and the dates that family members died; either by tomb sweeping, offering joss sticks, burning of paper money, or setting up altars, ancestral statues; painting; or wooden, paper tablet; offering of fruit, food, or wine, and animals. We even built temples or shrines for our ancestors, and worship our ancestors in public or through families formal rituals with singing, dancing, bowing and kow towing, bended knees...etc. also we have prayed and asked for ancestral spirits to come protect us, bless us, and bring peace. We set up shrines for the dead with food offerings and joss sticks, candles in funeral for people to worship, some even invite nuns and monks or Taoist priests to recite scriptures and perform ceremonies. I confess all these behaviors and customs as sins of believing in false religion, worship of dead and necromancy. Please forgive us of all our sins and cleanse us of all our unrighteousness.

In the name of Jesus Christ, I break and destroy all of these altars, shrines, temples, statues, paintings, photographs, tablets in the spiritual realm; I also cancel and break the power of all the rituals, ceremonies, worships, every offering, food, fruit, wine, joss sticks, paper money, urns, burners, candles, scriptures, spells, wooden fish, bells; all the words in asking, praying, wishing and vows; all the kow tow, bowing, kneeling, bending knees and declare them null and void, they no longer affect me. I break all covenants and agreements that have been established with the evil power of death and hell through all of these rituals, articles, materials, words and declare them null and void.

Thank You Jesus for forgiving me by shedding Your precious blood and cleansing all my unrighteousness. By my will, I now choose to forgive my parents, all my ancestors, friends and relatives, and all those who have influenced me in ancestral worship and worship of the dead, the persons who started this custom and those who spread them in the Chinese culture. I release each and every one of them into the freedom of my forgiveness, also release them from all debt they might owe me especially love and righteousness. In Jesus Christ's Holy name. Amen

In the name of Jesus Christ, I command all spirits of death and hell, all familiar spirits that my ancestors have invited, and evil spirits coming in through Kung-fu, Chi-kung, fortune-telling, fong-shui, and all spirit of curses that have come in because of war effects, catastrophes, disaster and victimization, torturing....

etc. I command you to go out from me and go to where Jesus takes you never to return or disturb anyone. I don't want you and do not belong to you, I belong to Jesus Christ and Jesus Christ alone. In Jesus Christ's name. Amen.

[Cancelling and Breaking of Blood /Covenant Curse of the Generational Line]

This is the ancestral legacy of the most fundamental sin

1.   Father, I come before You to confess and repent for my family sin as our ancestors may have made covenants with the devil and his cohorts with the oath of blood. I declare and renounce all of the vows that my ancestors have made to each enemy and evil spirit. I cancel the power of every word, every sentence and declare them null and void in the Holy Name of Jesus Christ.

2.   On behalf of my family, I confess for my ancestors' sin as they may have partaken in eating the human heart or human and animal sacrifices to false gods or evil spirits, and declared and announce all these sacrificial rituals, the offerings used, the use of knives, ritual implemented, the concept of prayer and so on to be null and void. In The holy name of Jesus Christ, I declare that all of these ceremonies and prayers as invalid and I break all the curses brought by these rituals and offerings and covenants.

3.   On behalf of my family, I confess and repent sins of my family ancestral lines that my ancestors may have drank human blood, performed cannibalism,

168

ate and drank the blood of animals, and using blood as offering to feed demons or as offering to worship the devil, false gods and evil spirits. I renounce and break all the effects of the shedding of innocent blood, drinking human blood, cannibalism, eating and drinking animals blood, and offering blood to demons in my ancestral lines and declare them null and void. In the name of Jesus Christ I break and cancel of all the curses brought by all these sins, especially the curses formed through blood rituals and offerings.

4.   On behalf of my family, I confess and repent that my ancestors may have done evil in Your sight by committing adultery in the temple of false idols asking and praying to idols in order to reproduce heirs or dedicating a child and descendants to idols or the dead in order to keep them healthy. In Jesus Christ's holy name I break and cancel all the curses brought by all these sins.

Father God, I come before You in the name of Jesus, confessing and renouncing these sins in my family lines. I now lay the punishment, curses and inherited weaknesses onto Jesus, my Scapegoat, on His bruised and broken body on the cross and release myself from their ill effects. Thank you, Lord, that I can cast my burdens on You.

By an act of my will, I unreservedly forgive my

ancestors for their sins and release my ancestors into the freedom of my forgiveness.

I confess and renounce my own sins in these areas, especially as they affect my family. I repent and turn from them and ask You to forgive and cleanse me with the precious blood of Jesus. Thank you, Lord Jesus, for cleansing me. Please heal me, renew me and lead me in Your way, Lord Jesus. Amen.

(Write and developed from teaching of Paul L. Cox Ministry)

[Prayer of Repentance for Chinese Zodiac and Dragon Worship]

Dear Abba Father, I confess that I and my family and ancestors have followed Chinese culture and traditions and believed that dragons were auspicious animals; through use of the Chinese lunar-solar calendar celebrated years associated with animal zodiac signs. I confess that this worship of animals as gods as sin. I also confess that I, my family and ancestors have used dragons in decorations, carvings, displays, furniture, homes, temples, shrines, pillars, roofs, embroidered on clothing, etc., and admit that all these are acts of inviting dragons into our home to be auspicious and protective charms. We used to call our emperor as "true dragon son of god" and have often wished our children to become dragons and phoenixes, had sayings of giving birth to dragon sons and dragon daughters, and have said that Chinese are descendants of the dragon. We have held dragon and tiger dances during festivals and celebrations, raced dragon boats during Duan Wu festival, etc., all these are acts of worshiping the dragon. I also confess that we used to believe in the 12 zodiac animals, and that I used to say that "My zodiac sign is _____", my parents, relatives, and friends also used to say that I am a _____. I also used to say other people had zodiac signs and believed in the characteristics associated with an animal, believed in unlucky years and Chinese astrological

171

calendar. I confess that these are all acts of worshiping Satan. "So the great dragon was cast out, that serpent of old, called the Devil and Satan" (Rev 12:9). Please forgive me and my family and ancestors, cleanse us of all unrighteousness. In the name of Jesus, I repent and cast away every traditional belief regarding dragons and animal zodiacs. I proclaim that I am not a descendant of the dragon and do not belong to the sign of _____; I belong to the Lord Jesus Christ, chosen by the Heavenly Father to become His son/daughter through the work of Jesus Christ. In Jesus' name, I cancel all words that I have heard and said regarding the Chinese zodiac and dragon, and proclaim that they are null and void. In Jesus' name, I bind and command all evil spirits associated with dragon and zodiac animals and (zodiac animal) to leave me, never to come back or hurt another person. In Jesus' name, Amen!

Lord Jesus, thank you for forgiving all my sins and cleansing me of all unrighteousness. By an act of my will, I choose to forgive my parents, ancestors, friends, and every person who influenced me to worship the dragon and believe in zodiac animals, including those who first started and spread these traditions. I forgive each of them into the freedom of my forgiveness, and free them of all the debts they might owe me, especially love and righteousness. In Jesus' name. Amen.

[Confess and Repent for Occult Sin]

Any past experience or activities you have involved in false religion and related activities, or any activities involved in power of darkness, or secrecy, you need to seriously to confess, repent and renounce: *(please refer to occult list.)*

[Confess and Repent for Occult Sin]

Dear Heavenly Father, I come before You CONFESSING, RENOUNCING and REPENTING of all sinful, occult practices and idolatry of seeking information, knowledge, healing, comfort, identity or power from any occult, psychic or secret source. I RENOUNCE all use of occult power, casting spells or witchcraft, voodoo, black and white magic and any other forms of local witchcraft. I CONFESS that I have sinned against You and Your Word by my involvement with the following occult practices _____(*speak out here all known involvement*). I acknowledge that ultimately all these practices are the worship of Satan and I choose now to REPENT and place Jesus Christ of Nazareth, Who came in the flesh, on the throne of my life. I ask You now to forgive me for these and any other occult involvement that I may have knowingly or unknowingly entered into and cleanse me of their effects on my family and me. In Jesus' name. Amen.

[Prayer of Forgive]

Thank You, Jesus, for dying that I might be forgiven. By an act of my will I now choose to forgive those who have influence me or forced me to the worship of other gods and involve me in occult practices._____ (Name out loud the people which need to be forgiven.) I release each and every one of these people into the freedom of my forgiveness. I release them from my judgments and from all debts they might owe me, especially love and righteousness. In Jesus' name. Amen.

[Forgiveness of oneself]

Thank You, Father, for forgiving me for things I have done. I now choose to forgive myself for the things which I know You have already forgiven me for. In Jesus' name. Amen.

[Renunciation of Satan's works]

Satan, I hereby renounce you and all your works in my life. I, by an act of my will and in the strength that Jesus Christ of Nazareth gives me, close the doors of my life at all the entry points you have previously gained through my sins. I speak out, in the name of Jesus who defeated you at Calvary that you no longer have any right to trouble me on these specific issues, which have now been confessed, repented of and forgiven, and from which I am now being cleansed by the shed blood of the Lord Jesus Christ.

In Jesus' name, I bind every evil spirit that related to the sins I have confessed and repented of. In the name of Jesus Christ, and by the power of His precious blood, I command every one of you to go out of me, go where Jesus takes you, never to return, never to hurt any human beings. In Jesus' name. Amen.

[Prayer to Break Occult power]

In the Holy name of Jesus Christ, I break and cancel everything that I and my ancestors and family members have done in idol worship including, the rituals, the altars and celebrations for various idols and the worship and the offerings (food, fruit, animals and watery alcohol), the use of incense burners, ritual implements, wooden fish, prayer flag, bamboo lots, Jiao-Gao, talisman, Fu, stuffed incense bags, incense ash water, money, burned paper money, candle lights, Joss ticks, the title or name of monk or nun they have received in false religion, the false religion scriptures and spells they recite, the name of various idols, every word they prayed, wishes, declarations, and vows they made with idols and evil powers. All kowtow, worship, worship in special hand statues, on bended knees, and all the benefits they received from demonic power. In the holy name of Jesus Christ, I declare them null and void. They can no longer affect me. I also cancel and break all the covenants and agreements they made with the devil and dark power behind all idols through these ceremonies, articles, materials used or offered, clothes, money, altars, statues and words written or declared and declare them null and void.

In the holy name of Jesus Christ, I break and cancel everything related to martial art (like Tai-Chi, Yoga, Karate, chi kung... etc.) that I and my ancestors and family members have undergone the training of. Including all kata of martial arts, every move, the body movements, meditation posture, hand posture, formula recitations, the Heart Sutra. I declare them null and void. In the holy name of Jesus Christ, I renounce all the ungodly believes that originated from martial arts, Chi and Kung-fu, especially of martial art that can strengthen the body and that has healing power and all powers that I and my ancestors and family members have received from practicing of martial art, Chi meditation, and Kung fu.

In the holy name of Jesus Christ I renounce all Taoism, Buddhism beliefs in witchcrafts, magic and supernatural power, including fortune-telling, divination, feng shui, (say out loud every time and form of fortune-telling, divination, feng shui you and your family and ancestors have been involved in), magic healing, acupuncture, chi-kung medical treatment, and demon driven ritual(including call back the dead, drinking ash water of fu, use of fu, talismans, call back lost soul due to fright, casting out demons using Taoist witchcraft, acupuncture, chi-kung healing). In the holy name of Jesus Christ I break and cancel all words that have been said through all fortune-tellers, medium on my ancestors and family members and off springs and declare them null and void. I also break and cancel all activities of alterations and objects and decoration materials, furnishings that my ancestors

177

and family have done due to believing in feng-shui, and all things and objects and talismans and fu used in demon driven rituals, every material and stuff (like hair, clothes, fu, spell, scripture, rice, blood, wine and _____ list any other item or material used before for rituals of cult practices)and power of evil spirits, I declare them to be null and void and can no longer affect me. I also cancel all covenants that the ancestors made with demonic power through these materials, fu, blood, wine, scripture and rituals and declare them to be null and void, no longer will affect me.

In the holy name of Jesus Christ I command all the evil spirits of all idols and all the evil and familiar spirits that my ancestors have invited as result of practicing martial arts, chi-kung, and the evil spirits they invited in because of the believe and practice of feng-shui, and fortune telling, and witch craft. I command all of you to go out of me. Go where the Lord Jesus Christ wants you to go, never to return, and never to come back again, and not to disturb anyone else. I do not need you; I do not belong to you. I belong to the Lord Jesus Christ and belong to Him alone. In Jesus Christ's Holy Name. Amen.

If any of my ancestors have become the priest of a false religion or idol, (e.g. monks, nun, Taoist priest, medium, temple care taker, fortune teller, or Confucianism scholar...etc.) or they have proselytize false religion like (selling or making figurines or statues of idol, joss sticks, paper money and other products for idol worship or used for rituals in false religion, building temple, play roles or music in the operas that promote stories of legend of false religion…etc.) In Jesus' name, I break all the power of these words and songs and activities, any rituals and vows, prayers, wishes, pronouncements that my ancestors made in the rituals of taking these priesthood positions; all the money, benefits, authorities and honors they received as false religion priest, and covenant they made with demonic power behind all these false religion, and declare it null and void. In Jesus' name, I also renounce all the name, fame and positions of false religion priest (name the name of the position and special priest name if you know). In Jesus' name I declare, I am a chosen by Father God, I am the royal priest of Kingdom of God, I am a people of God's kingdom, and resides in God's family.

In Jesus' name, I command all the evil spirits, demonic powers that are related to idols, false religion, and familiar spirits or ruling spirits that my ancestors and family members has invited; evil spirits that came in through Kong-fu, chi-kung; evil spirits that came in from practices of fortune telling, feng-shui, witchcraft, necromancy, connecting to evil power; evil spirits that came in through acupuncture, chi-kung healing and witchcraft healing; and all evil spirits that came in because of being false religious priest, and proselytizing false religion, I command all of you to go out of me, go where Jesus takes you, never to return, never to hurt any human being. I neither need you nor belong to you; I belong to Jesus, and Jesus along. In Jesus' name! Amen.

[Prayer of Defense Mechanism]

Father God, I confess due to the fear of rejection and being hurt, I have built a self-defense mechanism, walls and iron bars to protect myself. Father God I confess for the following defenses and reactions _____ (see attached form and other defenses you know of yourself). Father God, I confess these as sin and understand all these are also stumbling walls that I have put up, hindering my relationship with You. Now, I ask You to tear down all these bars and walls. I now free myself from all these encumbrances. Lord Jesus, I acknowledge You to be the Lord of every area of my life; I will not use these defense mechanisms to protect myself using my own strength but to depend on You. Lord Jesus, You are my strength, my shield, my shelter, my fortress, my refuge, my comforter. In Jesus' name. Amen.

[Self Defense System]

Flight	
Sulking	Disguise
Withdraw	Self center
Denial/Justify	Independence
Moodiness	Isolation
Introspection	Pessimism
Ultimate Right	Bitterness
Self-Pity	Inner vow
Self-destruction	Silence
Brokenness	Unbelief
Cynicism	Passiveness
Skepticism	Depression

[Self Defense System]

Flight	
Manipulation	Anger
Bitterroot	Blame Shift
Judgment	Pronouncement
Domination	Stubbornness
Control	Competition
Criticism	Perfectionism
Pride	Accusation
Hardness	Argumentative
Always right/	Harshness
Never wrong	Legalism
Violence	Sarcasm

[Prayer to Break Off from Ungodly Mind Set]

Father God, I confess that due to hurt or wrong teaching, or cultural back ground, I have believed in lies and have developed ungodly belief systems. I confess for the ungodly belief systems in Chinese/Eastern Asian culture, and lies about my Identity, value and destiny, including _____.

(Confess out loud about all the wrong beliefs, see ungodly belief system form)

I now know all these are lies, I confess and repent from it, and I invite Jesus Christ to be the Lord of all my belief system and my behavior cycles. I renounce all these wrong belief systems and cancel all the agreement with these lies. I choose Truth to replace all of these lies. Holy Spirit, please help me by freeing me from all these wrong belief systems, and plant Truth deep into my heart, and help me to break all the behavior cycles that have been built by these wrong belief system. May the words in my mouth and the meditation in my heart and all my behavior cycles to be pleasing in Your sight. Father God. In Jesus' name. Amen.

Lies	Chinese Traditional Mind Set
Stratification Dictatorship Confucianism	◆ Dictatorship, stratification, class division. ◆ Can't talk back to superior class ◆ Parents are right all the time ◆ Unconditional obedience to authority ◆ Children should not express self opinion, because they know nothing ◆ Children should only listen, no word or opinion ◆ Never praise children, shall they be proud or cursed ◆ Have to please authority figure ◆ Have to follow all the different behavior as ritual instruments

Lies	Chinese Traditional Mind Set
Perfectionism	◆ Needing to perform
	◆ Not allowed to fail
	◆ Cannot loose face
	◆ Have to glorify the ancestor and family's name
	◆ Have to be better than others
	◆ Criticize others and self, judgmental, self condemnation
	◆ No grace, no forgiveness, deserve punishment for failing, high expectations from parents and society
	◆ Comparison, competition, control, Manipulation, Power game, fighting for benefit

Lies	Chinese Traditional Mind Set
Perfectionism	• Fault finding to prove my capability • Expect others to be perfect or else one is not satisfied.
Confucianism	• Education system; High lifting knowledge. Everything has no value, except study • As long as having good academic results, you can do everything • Grades represents a person's value, achievements, and future • Forced feeding education, or "cramming" education (memorized learning) • Memorized study without understanding • Despise people of lower rank

Lies	Chinese Traditional Mind Set
Patriarchal ideology, Women is inferior of men	◆ Women's "three following law and four virtue" ◆ Submit to bad situation ◆ Pessimism, passiveness ◆ Unfilial three(no. one is that one must have a son as descendant or else dishonor parent), be without ◆ Need to have son to carry family name ◆ Children owe parents for raising them ◆ Raising children for old age

Lies	Chinese Traditional Mind Set
Suppression	◆ Suppress emotion, can't express properly ◆ Man do not cry easily ◆ Punishment is love; I punish you because of love. ◆ Deeper the love, heavier the discipline ◆ Well behave is good, well behaved only will be loved and accepted
Bondage of ancestor worship	◆ Not worship ancestor is disobeying parents ◆ Have to give birth to a son, then you will be worshiped after death. ◆ The eldest son have to bear the burden to worship ancestors

Lies	Chinese Traditional Mind Set
Idol worship False religion (Taoism, Buddhism)	• Yin-yang, five elements, fear toward the dark power of spiritual realm.
	• Worship of idol, animal figure, hero, dead, hell figure, legendary figure, Spiritism, Animism. Seclusion, immortal (fairies), Taoism practices.
	• Good deeds, good person
	• Assiduous, Buddhism practices.
	• Vegetarian, Retiracy, Reincarnation plot merit, Buddhism release life animal, eliminate karma (try to redeem sin by self effort)
	• Use meditation and Zen practices

Lies	Chinese Traditional Mind Set
Idol worship False religion (Taoism, Buddhism)	◆ Suppress emotion, worry. ◆ Nothing concrete (everything is empty) (sì dà jiē kōng) ◆ Nirvana mode, selfless, non-existing ◆ Self practice to become Buddha, holiness. Fruition ◆ Practice Kong-fu, Tai-Ji ,Chi-gong to be strengthen in physical body, or to be healed ◆ Fortune telling, spiritual reading ◆ Taoist healing method, acupuncture, chi-gong ◆ Taoist ritualistic deliverance ◆ Good luck day

Lies	Chinese Traditional Mind Set
Dependent, performance, Hypocrite, Mask with polite word	◆ Face saving, afraid of losing face ◆ Shame, bashful ◆ I have to be a good Christian, I can't let God lose face ◆ In order to complete my job, I have to neglect my own needs. ◆ I have to work hard in order to please others, to receive applause from others, only I can be good Christian. ◆ I can't let others know my weakness ◆ I have to have good result to show to God. ◆ Can't say sorry

Lies	Chinese Traditional Mind Set
Dependent, performance, Hypocrite, Mask with polite word	◆ Not wash your dirty linen in public: I should never mention my family problems to anybody else.
Valueless (Useless,Not important, unworthy, not measure up, insignificant) pessimism	◆ I am a mistake, I shouldn't even be born. ◆ If I need help, I am troubling others. ◆ My thought is not important, not even worth to mention. ◆ Nobody will notice my existence. ◆ My needs is not important ◆ I have no need ◆ I am bad luck, nothing good will happen on me.

Lies	Chinese Traditional Mind Set
Valueless (Useless, Not important, unworthy, not measure up, insignificant) pessimism	◆ I am lousy, I will not succeed ◆ Life is miserable, bad things happen often.
Domination, control, manipulation, Jezebelic mind	◆ I have to control and make sure everything in place, otherwise I am irresponsible. ◆ Parent is always right, I punish him for his benefit. ◆ Lack of Godly boundary ◆ Not honoring others opinion, free will, and rights. ◆ Not listening to me, is dishonoring me.

Lies	Chinese Traditional Mind Set
Ultimate right Self-righteousness Pride Intellective	◆ I am that I am, I don't need to change ◆ I can't change, Mountains and nation can change, but a person's character can't change I can't be wrong, I have to be right ◆ Old dog never learn new tricks ◆ I am always right, blame shift. ◆ Nervousness, Anxiety, Worry.
Fear	◆ Fear of man. ◆ Fear of Authority. ◆ Fear of punishment. ◆ Fear of making mistake ◆ Fear of loosing face

Lies	Chinese Traditional Mind Set
Fear	• Fear of rejection • Fear of failure, Fear of disapproval • Fear of danger, fear of hurt • Fear of illness
Suppression of emotions	• Real Man don't cry • Turning grief and anger into strength and determination • I shall never cry again • Crying is no use/ Crying only brings trouble • Anger is a bad behavior • Crying portray weakness, with which no one will sympathize

Lies	Chinese Traditional Mind Set
Suppression of emotions	◆ I have no right to be angry ◆ Anger is not womanly ◆ A good Christian shouldn't be angry ◆ Anger portrays immaturity ◆ Anger is wrong, I must control myself not to show anger. ◆ Anger is terrifying
Poverty	◆ Fear of poverty, fear of lack, fear of lost, nervousness, anxiety, insecurity related to war effect. ◆ Can't trust the Lord, worry of lack, have to tightly control all the resources ◆ Opportunist, take advantage of others

Lies	Chinese Traditional Mind Set
Poverty	◆ Fear of poverty, fear of lack, fear of lost, nervousness, anxiety, insecurity related to war effect. ◆ Can't trust the Lord, worry of lack, have to tightly control all the resources ◆ Opportunist, take advantage of others ◆ Fear of short by others, stingy, ◆ Calculative, petty ◆ Short change of other's ◆ Greedy, robbery, always trying to identify loop holes for self gain ◆ Money can do everything ◆ Despising poor

(Above ungodly belief system was gathered through the revelation from Holy Spirit. Since everyone has different back ground, each person's belief system may vary. Please seek the guidance from Holy Spirit to reject and renounce all the ungodly belief system, especially those from Chinese cultural back ground, Confucianism, Buddhism, Taoism, War effect...etc. Ask the Lord to deliver you from all these strong holds)

[Prayer for the Cutting of Generational Ties]

I. **Cut off**-cutting of generational ties of father and father's family line, mother and mother's family line.

I unreservedly forgive all my ancestors for every ungodly thing they have done that have brought ill effects in my life, I confess and renounce every sin that my ancestors committed before, especially (confess those sins that you know).

In the name of Father, Son and Holy Spirit, I break all ungodly generational spirit, soul and body links that are in between _____'s father and ancestors in _____ father's family line and _____'s mother and mother's family line (and also ancestral line in _____ spouse' family). In Jesus' name I break these linking supernaturally, and I ask that You, Father God to remove from_____ every effect of _____'s ancestor's sins and every part of them which has been wrongfully tied in bondage to _____ and remove from _____ all ungodly influence, curse or weakness which came from them. I ask You, Lord to return to _____ every part of _____ which has been wrongfully tied in bondage to _____'s ancestors. I ask You, Father, to place the cross of Jesus and His shed blood between _____ and _____'s father's family line and _____'s mother's family line and stop all ungodly things from flowing in between them and _____, cover, cleanse and cancel all rights and curses and influences from these sins and iniquities. I ask You to allow blessings, but to stop the curses. I declare that _____ is free from all the curses, judgments and consequences, and inherited diseases that resulting from the ancestor sins and iniquities. In Jesus' Name! Thank You Jesus! You have died and shed Your precious blood for _____, and Your body was crucified, bruised and broken for _____, You became curse and _____ can receive blessing, You delivered _____ and set _____ free, You have turned all curses from generational lines into double blessings for _____. Amen.

II. If you and your family or ancestors had customs of ancestral worship (Necromancy), then you need to deal with the influences that are caused by ancestral spirit that have been bonded by this custom.

[Prayer to set ancestral spirit free from bondage]

In Jesus name, I take authority over every demonic spirits that came in through ancestor worship, I command you to stand down and be quiet. In the name of Father, Son and Holy Spirit, I break all the linking in between all demonic spirits and ancestral spirits. In

Jesus' name I commit all _____'s ancestral spirits into the hands of Jesus Christ, you can go where Jesus wants you to go, and go in peace. Father God, I ask You to send ministering angels to come and help us, separate all demonic spirit with ancestral spirit, and lead every ancestral spirit to the hands of Jesus. In Jesus' name. Amen.

III. Cast out all related demonic spirit

In Jesus' Name, I bind every demonic spirit that come from _____'s generational line and is influencing _____, I command you to go out of _____, go where Jesus takes you, never to return, never to hurt any human being again. Father God, I ask You to send ministering angels to help us, arrest and bind every demonic spirit that is influencing _____, sent them to where Jesus wants them to go, never to return, never to hurt any human being again. Amen.

[Breaking generational curses in Deuteronomy 28:15-68]

In Jesus' name, I break curses that have come done from my ancestral and generational line.

1. I break all curses in the city and curses in the country.

2. I break all curses against my basket and my kneading bowl (my bank account and my earning power).

3. I break all curses against the fruit of my body and the produce of my land, the increase of my cattle and the offspring of my flocks.

4. I break all curses against us when we come in, and when we go out.

5. I repent for all the wickedness of my family doings in which we have forsaken the LORD. I renounce and break all curses, confusion, and rebuke in all that my family set our hand to do, I renounce and break all destruction and sudden perish in my family.

6. I break all curses of plagues cling to my family until we were consumed from the land which we are going to possess.

7.   I break all curses of my family being strike with consumption, with fever, with inflammation, with severe burning fever, with the sword, with scorching, and with mildew; and curses of my family being pursued by them until we perish.

8.   I break all curses of heavens over our head being bronze, and the earth under us being iron.

9.   I break all curse of the rain of our land turning into powder and dust from the heaven and coming down on us until we are destroyed.

10.   I break all curse of my family being defeated before our enemies; we go out one way against them and flee seven ways before them; and I renounce and break the curse of my family becoming troublesome to all the kingdoms of the earth.

11.   I break all curses of our carcasses becoming food for all the birds of the air and the beasts of the earth and no one to frighten them away.

12.   I break all curses of my family being stricken with the boils of Egypt, with tumors, with the scab, and with the itch, from which we cannot be healed.

13.   I break all curses of my family being stricken with madness and blindness and confusion of heart.

14.   I break all curses that we grope at noonday, as a blind man gropes in darkness; and we cannot prosper in our ways; we were only oppressed and plundered continually, and no one can save us.

15.   I break all curses that we betroth a wife, but another man lie with her; we build a house, but cannot dwell in it; we plant a vineyard, but cannot gather its grapes.

16.   I break all curses that our ox being slaughtered before our eyes, but we cannot eat of it; our donkey being violently taken away from before us, and cannot be restored to us; our sheep being given to our enemies, and we have no one to rescue them.

17.   I break all curses that our sons and our daughters being given to another people, and our eyes look and fail with longing for them all day long; and we have no strength in our hand.

18.   I break all curses that A nation whom we have not known eating the fruit of our land and the produce of our labor, and we were only oppressed and crushed continually (Others rubbed my benefit from what I labored).

19.   I renounce and break that we were driven mad because of the sight which our eyes see.

20. I break all curses that we were stricked in the knees and on the legs with severe boils which cannot be healed, and from the sole of our foot to the top of our head.

21. I break all curses that we were brought to the king whom we set over us to a nation which neither us nor our fathers have known, and there we serve other gods—wood and stone.

22. I break all curses that we become an astonishment, a proverb, and a byword among all nations where the LORD drove us.

23. I break all curses that we carry much seed out to the field but gather little in, for the locust consumed it.

24. I break all curses that we plant vineyards and tend them, but we can neither drink of the wine nor gather the grapes; for the worms will eat them.(we cannot benefit from our labor)

25. I break all curses that we have olive trees throughout all our territory, but we cannot anoint ourselves with the oil; for our olives will drop off. (curse of unable to reap what you sow)

26. I break all curses that we beget sons and

daughters, but they are not ours; for they went into captivity.

27.   I break all curses that locusts consume all our trees and the produce of our land.

28.   I renounce and break the alien who is among us rise higher and higher above us, and we come down lower and lower.

29.   I renounce and break the curse that others lend to us, but we cannot lend to them; they will be the head, and we will be the tail.

30.   I renounce and break the curse that all these curses come upon us and pursue and overtake us, until we are destroyed, because we did not obey the voice of the LORD our God, to keep His commandments and His statutes which He commanded us. I renounce and break the curse that they will be upon us for a sign and a wonder, and on our descendants forever.

31.   I confess and repent that we did not serve the LORD our God with joy and gladness of heart, for the abundance of everything, Lord! Please forgive us for our sin.

32.   I break all curses that we will serve our enemies, whom the LORD send against us, in hunger,

in thirst, in nakedness, and in need of everything; I renounce and break the curse of a yoke of iron on our neck until being destroyed.

33.　　I renounce and break the curse that a nation against us from afar, from the end of the earth, as swift as the eagle flies, a nation whose language we will not understand, a nation of fierce countenance, which does not respect the elderly nor show favor to the young.

34.　　I break all curses that they eat the increase of our livestock and the produce of our land, until we are destroyed; they will not leave us grain or new wine or oil, or the increase of our cattle or the offspring of our flocks, until we were destroyed.

35.　　I break all curses that they besiege us at all our gates until our high and fortified walls, in which we trust, come down throughout all our land; and they will besiege us at all our gates throughout all our land which the LORD our God has given us.

36.　　I renounce and break the curse that we will eat the fruit of our own body, the flesh of our sons and our daughters whom the LORD our God has given us, in the siege and desperate straits in which our enemy shall distress us.

37.　　I renounce and break the curse that the

sensitive and very refined man among us will be hostile toward his brother, toward the wife of his bosom, and toward the rest of his children whom he leaves behind. (Family members resent and against each other)

38.   I renounce and break the curse that man will not give any of them the flesh of his children whom he will eat, because he has nothing left in the siege and desperate straits in which our enemy distress us at all our gates.

39.   I renounce and break the curse of the tender and delicate woman among us, who would not venture to set the sole of her foot on the ground because of her delicateness and sensitivity, will refuse the husband of her bosom, and to her son and her daughter,

40.   I renounce and break the curse that woman eat secretly her placenta which comes out from between her feet and her children whom she bears; for lack of everything in the siege and desperate straits in which our enemy distress us at all our gates.

41.   I renounce and break the curse that because we do not carefully observe all the words of God's law that are written in this book, that we may fear this glorious and awesome name, THE LORD OUR GOD, then the LORD brought upon our ancestors and descendants extraordinary plagues—great and prolonged plagues—

and serious and prolonged sicknesses.

42.   I renounce and break the curse that the Lord bring back on us all the diseases of Egypt, of which we were afraid, and they will cling to us.

43.   I renounce and break the curse that every sickness and every plague, which *is* not written in this Book of the Law, were brought upon us until we were destroyed.

44.   I renounce and break the curse that we will left few in number,   because we did not obey the voice of the LORD your God.

45.   I renounce and break the curse that we will be plucked from off the land which we go to possess. I renounce and break the curse that we were scattered among all peoples, from one end of the earth to the other, and there we serve other gods, which neither us nor our fathers have known—wood and stone.

46.   I renounce and break the curse that we among those nations we find no rest, nor shall the sole of our foot have a resting place; but there the LORD will give us a trembling heart, failing eyes, and anguish of soul.

47.   I renounce and break the curse that our life hanging in doubt before us; we will fear day and night,

and have no assurance of life. In the morning you shall say, 'Oh that it were evening!' And at evening you shall say, 'Oh, that it were morning!' because of the fear which terrifies your heart, and because of the sight which your eyes see.

48.   I renounce and break the curse that we were taken back to Egypt in ships, and there we will be offered for sale to our enemies as male and female slaves, but no one will buy us."

[Breaking curses on Finances in the family lines]

I the name of Jesus I repent for all evil deeds of my own and my ancestors that has cursed finances in my family line and in my life. I repent for, and renounce all the wrong belief systems lies and behavior.

In Jesus' name, I repent and renounce, that either I and my family has done

1.   Exchange of funds done in ungodly ways, (money exchange, ex. White wash...)

2.   Money spent on sinful way...ex. prostitutes, gambling.

3.   Those that did not tithe (and I ask you Lord to break the devourer off my line). Those who did not serve the Lord our God joyfully and gladly in the time of prosperity (Deut. 28:47)

4.   Those who worship false religion and idols. Those who helped fund or those who spent money in false religion. Those using witchcraft to make money, selling products that used for false religion or idol worship.

5.   Greed, Worshipping of money and the "love of

money" (1 Tim. 6:10). Those who trusted in money and self-effort above trusting in God. Materialism, money worshiper.

6.   Those who sold their souls to gain finances.

7.   Merciless to neighbor or others: Stingy; Those that did not care for the poor; Those who oppressed the poor; Opportunist; to do shoddy work and use inferior material; to scamp work and stint material; to jerry-build, take advantage of others; Calculative; petty; Short change other's; short of other's wages. Unpaid wages – (James 5:4). Not Forgiving debts – (Matthew 6:12)

8.   Leaders who unjustly taxed the poor. Ungodly usury (Ps 15:5, Ex 22:25)

9.   Ungodly ways of gaining money... steal, drug trafficking, human trafficking, slave trading, taking money from people to hurt others, ex. assassin, false testimonies...etc. Bribes taken against the innocent (Ps. 15:5) Using violent force to collect debts. Those who sold Christian relics for money. Ungodly agreements with the enemy to obtain finances. Those who commit adultery-(Proverbs 5:10)

10.   As a professional beggar, lived beggar's life and made covenant with poverty.

11.   Vows of poverty that were made and or broken (monks & priests may have taken and broken vows of poverty, which would have put a curse on the finances of future generations)

12.   Mercenary Acts.

13.   Leprechaun spirits (trickery and false promising of money)

14.   All kind of curses in finance: Those who shed innocent blood; the curse of wandering; restlessness; (Orig. from Cain in Gen. 4:12); Witchcraft curses against finances; All curses of bankruptcy; Curses on actual money that has given to me; untimely death, traumatic death, accidental sudden death; cursed to be unable to enjoy the fruit of labor; curses brought because of dishonoring parents (Exodus 20:12, Ephesians 6:2); covetous over other's properties. (Exodus 20:17)

15.   Giving to a ministry not ordained by the Lord, not following godly principle. (See purifying the altar by Al Houghton www.wordatwork.org)

In Jesus' name I declare them null and void, they will no longer influence me and my descendants. In Jesus' name, I cancel all assignments of the spirit of curses, I declare that I am free from all curses and enter into blessings that God has promised me.

In Jesus' name, I bind and command all evil spirit that has come against me from my family line to leave and go to the feet of Jesus to be assigned where He sends them to go, never to return and never to influence any other person. Father God, Please send your ministering spirit, warring angels to help me and complete all the prayers I have done. In Jesus' name. Amen.

(Revised from Paul L. Cox Ministry by Sozo Ministries Inc)

[Prayer for Lust and Sexual Sins]

[Prayer for sex related Sins]

Dear Father God, I confess during different periods in my life, I have not been able to defend against the enemy's continuous attacks, in the following situation I have chosen to sin. I ask for your forgiveness, I have... [say out loud and confess the sins Holy Spirit has revealed to you, for example: adultery, sex before marriage, outside of marriage or test marriages, Incest, Anal sex, oral sex (not including foreplay part), SM (of bundled games), Masochism, Sadism, misogyny addiction, fetishism, pedophilia, pornography movies online, telephone and network road sex, masturbation, Voyeurism disease (see other people's sex), bestiality, homosexuality, bisexuality, transvestite, transvestites, transgender people, rape, sexual assault.] I agree to your judgment toward my sins, I confess and repent these sins and the enjoyment from them. I ask you to remove all of the memories related to them, heal my wounds and forgive me. In the name of Jesus I pray. Amen.

[Repentance from Sexual Sins]

Father God, I come before you in the name of Jesus, I admit the sexual sins I have committed. My body, soul and spirit all sinned against you. You said if I confess my sins, you are faithful and righteous, and You will

216

forgive me, and cleanse me of my sins and all the guilt, shame, and feeling of dirtiness it has brought. Please let your living water flow through me and allow me to be cleansed.

From today forward, I choose to walk in your holiness, and let you be the Lord of my sexual desires and sexual activities. I am willing, under the power of the Holy Spirit, to choose to follow your holy words and command, whether in my sex life or any area of my life. I ask the Holy Spirit to help me, to walk in the way of the Lord, and obey the leading of the Holy Spirit. I declare I am willing to be a righteous person in all things including all relationships with the other gender/sex; and declare by the help of God, I will maintain a pure heart. In the name of Jesus, Amen.

[Declaration of God's forgiveness]

John 1, 1:9-If we confess our sins, he is faithful and just and will forgive us our sins and purify us from all unrighteousness.

[Forgiveness of Self]

Thank you Father for forgiving me, I now choose to forgive myself, I forgive myself of all the things You have forgiven me of. In the name of Jesus. Amen.

[Prayer of Forgiveness]

Forgive every sexual partners

Lord Jesus, thank you for dying on the cross for me, so that my sins are forgiven. By the act of my will, I now choose to forgive (name out those) who have influenced me in an ungodly way in my life, I release each and every one of them into the freedom of my forgiveness. I also release them from my judgment and any debt they owe me, especially in love. In the name of Jesus. Amen.

[Prayer to renounce Satan's work]

Satan, I now renounce all of you and your work in my life. By the act of my will and the power of Jesus of Nazareth, I close these doors to you forever. I command you in the name of Jesus, do not disturb me in these areas. I have confessed, repented, and forgive. I have been cleansed by the blood of Jesus Christ. Amen.

Any demonic spirits that are related to the sins I have confessed, in the name of Jesus, I bind you, and by the power of Jesus' name and his blood, I command you evil spirits to leave my life. Do not return. In the name of Jesus. Amen.

[Forgive the Abuser]

Lord Jesus, you know everything that has happened to me, you know the abandonment I felt, the loneliness, rejection, the abuse of my body and mind, and my crushed spirit, all of the pain and emotions I am struggling with because of the people/person who abused me. Please help me to be able to forgive those who hurt me from the bottom of my heart, please give me the courage to face these painful experiences, and become willing to give you all the pain and hurt I have. Lord, I choose to forgive _____ (mention the event and the person who hurt you sexually) I release them into the freedom of my forgiveness. I also release them from my judgment and any debt they owe me, especially in love and justice. In the name of Jesus, Amen.

[Cut spirit, Soul, Body Ties between Sex Partners or Abusers]

In the name of Jesus, I take up the sword of the Holy Spirit to cut all the ungodly spirit, soul, body ties between me and _____, in Jesus' holy name, I cut away all of these supernatural connections, and ask Father God to return to me what belongs to me, and whatever from _____ (name) back to _____, (name) and remove all the ungodly influences from_____ (name).

In the name of Jesus I declare, all of the related people, things, event, and power of darkness cannot affect me anymore. Lord Jesus, thank you for helping me to put down all of the bitterness and the desire of revenge, thank you for removing my stone heart, defense mechanism, bitterness, and help me to open the gates of my heart to receive you. Please fill me with your unconditional love and abundance, anoint me with the anointing of Gilead, Holy Spirit fill me and renew me, Jesus' blood cleanse me and set me apart in holiness.

Thank you for helping me to gain freedom from my past hurt, and enter into your abundant life. I pray this in thankfulness and Lord's victorious name. Amen.

[Note]Due to the sensitive nature of the sexual abuse cases, those who are abused tend to receive severe wounds, crushed spirit and broken hearts, the abused one will need a good amount of release of emotions and healing. If it was a light degree of harassment, the person may pray this on his/her own. If the event has left a deep scar or shadow in the person's life, affecting even the perspective of life, altered self-worth, or people who have mood swings, unsteady emotions should not pray this on their own or attempt to cast out demons on their own. It is advised they seek help from experienced staff in inner healings, these kinds of conditions will require deep inner healing and deliverance to completely heal.

[Prayer for the Sin of Abortion]

[Confess (Acknowledge Self Iniquities)]

Dear Father God, I confess life started from the time of conception, and abortion is an act of rubbing the rights of living from the fetus, is also a sin of murder. I confess the sin that I have committed of killing my own child, please forgive me.

I confess I have _____(Speak out loud so you hear yourself, all the sins you have committed about abortion, let Holy spirit to lead you on every event related to abortion, including all the details of reason, place and people who influence you. Let the person who is ministering to you to be the wittiness for you, so that enemy can't accuse you anymore. James 5:16). Father God, now I know I have sinned against You, I repent from this selfish sinful act, I confess that I don't have enough strength to overcome all the attacks and oppression from the enemy in areas where I am weak, inclusive of: my mind, emotion, and my behavior, however I chose to sin. I repent and turn away from this sin, please forgive me and cleanse me. Dear Father God, You are the creator of all things, and my life giver. Please forgive me for killing the life and blessings you have predestined. I need Your grace of forgiveness and peace of Jesus Christ. Please erase my iniquities according to Your abundant mercy, grace

221

and kindness. Please cleanse me from the shedding of innocent blood with the blood of Jesus Christ and wash me whiter than snow.

[Receive forgiveness and Healing from God]

By the blood of Jesus and the sacrifices he offered on the Cross. 1 John 1:9 says: *"If we confess our sins, He is faithful and just to forgive us our sins and to cleanse us from all unrighteousness."*

[Forgive others] (People who make you uncomfortable, or influence you, convince you or pressure you to make decision to abort baby)

Lord Jesus, thank you for dying for me, that I can be forgiven. Now, by an act of my will, I choose to forgive those who have influence me with ungodly influences (Let Holy spirit to lead you to speak out those who made you feel hurt, pain, fear, anxiety, insecurity during the process of making decision and abortion process, especially your sexual partner, staffs and doctors in the clinic or hospital, parents, authority figure, peers...etc.

◆ Sexual partner: _____ (name the name)

◆ Partner that decide or suggested or encouraged you to abort the baby_____(name the person) I forgive

222

you, when I needed your support and encouragement, you suggested or (requested) me to abort, and did not care for the baby that was unborn, and all the wound and hurt you have caused me during this process (speak out to the Lord about your feelings of hurt and thoughts).

◆ Partner was not able to help or support, or take responsibility, or change the circumstances_____ (name the name): I forgive you for not being able to change the circumstances to take responsibilities for me and the unborn child. I chose to forgive you and bless you, I pray that the Lord will forgive you and help you to receive the grace of salvation.

◆ Doctor, executer and staffs in clinic or hospital: _____(name their name or place, city or name of the hospital) Doctors and medical staff whoever was involved in this abortion process, I forgive you for giving me medicine or surgery to abort my baby, I understand that you may have thought you were helping me, but did not know that you caused me to sin. I also forgive you for not giving me advice or suggestions to help me to keep the child and avoid sinning.

◆ Parents or teacher or authority figure: _____ (name the name or title of the person) I forgive you for not understanding my problem, for not concerning yourself with me, and not asking about my difficulties, even pressured me or persuaded me to choose abortion.

◆ Friend or peers: _____(name their names or title) , I forgive you for being my friend but did not give me good advice when I needed, instead suggested me to abort or try to tell me this is the only and one way to resolve the problem, I forgive you for giving me wrong suggestions and led me to sin.I release each and every one of them into the freedom of my forgiveness. I release them from all my judgments and complaints and all the debts they might owe me, especially love. In Jesus' name. Amen.

[Forgive Oneself]

Father God, I thank you for Your word, 1 John 1:9 *"If we confess our sins, He is faithful and just to forgive us our sins and to cleanse us from all unrighteousness."* Psalm 51:17 The sacrifices of God are a broken spirit, a broken and a contrite heart— these, O God, You will not despise.

Thank You Abba Father! As I confess and repent of my sin, and by the grace through the sacrifice of Jesus Christ, You forgave all my sin and cleanse all my unrighteousness. Lord Jesus Christ, please cleanse me all my thoughts and memories, heal all the pain and hurt of my spirit, soul and body, and help me to forgive myself. I now choose to forgive myself according to the way You have forgiven me, and accept myself again, not to accuse or condemn or punish myself anymore. The chastisement for my peace was upon You, and by Your stripes I am healed. Lord Jesus, I now cast all my burden of negative emotions from this sin to You, all my _____ (name the negative emotions you have ex. Guilt, shame, regret, remorse, anxiety, confusion, heaviness, insecurity, self-condemnation, anger, rage, loneliness, fear, weakness, grief, depression, oppression...etc.), thank You Lord Jesus for care for me, to take all my emotional burden and pressure (release all emotions to the Lord). I receive the supernatural peace and freedom from you.

[Offer the Unborn Baby to the Lord]

Note: If you have offered the unborn baby to an idol(s), or made tablet as worship of dead baby, do this prayer first: Lord Jesus, I confess before I know You, I have sinned against you by offering my child to the idol(s) _____ (name of the idol or idols), or worship the dead baby, please forgive me and cleanse all my unrighteousness. (Use *"Prayer of breaking power of the Occult"* to break all the agreement made with ritual, prayer, offering, instrument, materials...)

In the name of Father, Son, and Holy Spirit, I savor all the spirit, soul and body linking in between my child and _____ (idols' name, or the altar of dead baby).

In Jesus' name, I cut this linking supernaturally, and ask Father God to bring back every part of my child back, and remove all the evil influences that come from all this idols and altar (name the idol or altar), also please sent Your warrior angels to complete all this works that I prayed).

Lord Jesus, I commit my child's spirit into Your hand, the Lamb of God, You are the great shepherd, You shall surely shepherd my baby, bring him to the fountain of life. "And God will wipe away every tear from their eyes; there shall be no more death, nor sorrow, nor crying. There shall be no more pain, for the former things have passed away." (Rev. 21:4). You have turned for me my mourning into dancing; You have put off my sackcloth and clothed me with gladness, To the end that my glory may sing praise to You and not be silent. O LORD my God, I will give thanks to You forever. (Psalm 30:11-12) Praise and glory be to the Lamb of God! In Jesus' name. Amen.

[Prayer to relate to Abortion]

1.   **For those unborn baby and mother:** Lord Jesus! Please strengthen those mothers who are struggling with the choice between abortion or not. Help them to trust in Your mercy and grace, to receive the gift of life You have given to them, so that they can treasure the life. The baby can be saved by their final

226

decision. Lord Jesus! Please comfort all these unborn babies' heart, to have them rest in your love and grace and receive supernatural peace.

2.   Mothers who abort and lost their baby: Lord Jesus! We ask for your grace and mercy for those mothers who cannot raise their own child for any reason, also please comfort their hearts. Lord Jesus, You have compassion for these mothers, who rejected their baby. Show them Your will and help them to know the truth and turn away from sin. As well as receive your redemption and grace and reconciliation with You.

3.   Aborted baby: Lord Jesus, We commit this unborn baby into Your hand, please bless them with Your love and comfort. Bind all the evil spirits that are binding them, break all bondages, set them free, deliver them from darkness so they enter into Your light and everlasting Kingdom.

4.   Medical doctors /staff and officers involved: Lord Jesus, we ask that You will enlighten those doctors and medical staff who are involved in the surgical procedures of abortion. We ask You to remove all the veils that blind them, restore their soul, open their eyes to see, ears to hear, heart to be clear, so they turn back to You. Let them use the talent, skill, knowledge and gifts You gave to them in godly ways to save lives. Also, help them to know and believe in Your love and mercy, to receive Your redemptive grace and mercy, forgive themselves and turn back to You. Bless every one of them to be a person who acts justly, love mercy and to walk humbly with You. Everyone do not delight in evil but rejoice with the truth.

5.   **Those who give abortion advice:** Lord Jesus, let Your light of truth shine upon those who gave advice or suggest abortion, remove all lies and darkness in their hearts, and let them know that You treasure every life, as well as know that life starts from conception. Make them treasure life as much as You do. Guard their hearts, above all else.

6.   **Pro-life workers:** Lord Jesus, Anoint Your servants who are pro-life workers, release resources, wisdom, power and courage unto them, and enlarge their territory. Let their ministry be like light that shines upon every dark corner of grief and sorrow; protect the rights of those unborn, and their life.

7.   **Law maker:** Lord Jesus, shine Your light on those officers who are involved in making laws which control population, women's right, health and social problems. I ask for a supernatural turn around, create an environment around them so they will know and learn Your will about life, so they too will come to treasure life and protect life, even the unborn ones.

[Prayer to Break Inner Vows]

Father God, I confess that I have made inner vows before, I said that _____. I now repent and cancel these vows. In the Name of Jesus Christ, I cancel _____ and declare them null and void; they can no longer affect me. By the sword of the Holy Spirit I separate myself from these vows and release myself from all the ill effects of these vows. In Jesus' name. Amen.

[Prayers to Break Bitter Root Judgments]

Father God, I confess that I have made Bitter root Judgments and expectations toward _____, I said that _____. I now repent and cancel these bitter root judgments and expectations. In the Name of Jesus Christ, I cancel _____ and declare them null and void; they can no longer affect me. By the sword of the Holy Spirit I separate myself from these bitter root Judgments and expectations, and release myself from all the ill effects of these bitter root Judgments and expectations. I replace all these bitter root Judgments and expectations with Truth, I choose to believe and agree with Truth that _____ In Jesus' name. Amen.

[Forgiveness Prayer]

Thank You, Jesus, for dying that I might be forgiven.

By an act of my will I now choose to forgive those who have hurt me. (Name out loud the people who need to be forgiven) I release each and every one of these people into the freedom of my forgiveness. I release them from my judgments and from all debts they might owe me, especially love. In Jesus' name. Amen.

[Prayer to Break off from Other's Judgments and Curses]

Lord Jesus, thank you for dying that I might be forgiven. By an act of my will I now choose to forgive those who have hurt me through curses and those who have wrongfully judged me, I forgive _____(Name out loud the people who need to be forgiven) I release each and every one of these people into the freedom of my forgiveness. In Jesus' name and the sword of Holy Spirit, I cut myself free from all these wrong judgments and curses _____ (name all the curses and wrong judgments from what people said to you), I declare them null and void, and they no longer have any ill effect over my life. In Jesus' name, Amen.

[Forgiveness of oneself]

Thank You, Father, for forgiving me for things that I have done. I now choose to forgive myself for the things that I know You have already forgiven me. I accept myself just as I am as the way You have accepted me. In Jesus' name. Amen.

[Prayer of confession for blaming God]

I confess that I have blamed You, Lord, for things that are not Your responsibility. I recognize this to be sin and I ask You to forgive me. I know that You hate what

Satan has done in my life. Thank You for loving me and promising to set me free. In Jesus' name.

[Renounce Satan's Work]

Satan, I hereby renounce you and all your works in my life. I, by an act of my will and in the strength that Jesus Christ of Nazareth gives me, close the doors of my life to all the entry points you have previously gained through my sins. I speak out, in the name of Jesus who defeated you at Calvary that you no longer have any right to trouble me on these specific issues, which have now been confessed, repented of, and forgiven, and from which I am now being cleansed by the shed blood of the Lord Jesus Christ.

[Note] After these prayers, use cleansing prayer, to cut all ungodly spirit, soul and body linkings. Take authority over the evil spirit; in Jesus' name command all spirit of bitterness, judgments, and curses to leave and cancel all the assignments of the enemy. In Jesus' name command every part of your spirit, soul, body, which were being affected by curses or judgments to re-align according to God's created order and restore back to what God originally created for you.

[Prayer To Receive Healing of the Uterus Experience]

When use this prayer, if you don't have any emotional release, do not push yourself too hard. Just deal with your mind set first, you can have some degree of healing, but still need to seek for deep healing, unless you know that you were not damaged in the womb. When a person who manifest severely when there is strong presence of the Holy Spirit , and is unable to control his/her body and action, It's always better to have another person (sister or brother in the Lord or another person you can trust) to accompany you, never do it alone. This is to avoid over reaction and secondary trauma. (If there are over reactions and the person loses control, the companion person should call the person's name and call back the person into consciousness, and do not continue) Seek the Lord's guidance for proper and experienced minister's help for further healing.

Lord Jesus, please help me and lead me, open my heart and my eyes, reveal to me all the damages in the womb experience from the time I was conceived to the time I was born. Lord, please wrap me around with your presence and love; help and lead me back to the memory of my womb experience. Lord! Please shine Your light in every corner of darkness in my spirit and soul, let your healing power touch every wound and hurting area in my deepest inner being, and let Your love fill me. Show me and reveal to me what has happened, let Truth be reveal, and the light shine upon every darkness in my heart, so that I may see every event through Your eyes. Your truth breaks all the bondages caused by the lies of the enemy, and I chose Your truth and reject the enemy's lies. In Jesus' name, I bind all the evil spirits surrounding me during the time of my mother's pregnancy and sever all the spiritual links between me (0-9 month in the womb) and all the evil spirits. Holy Spirit, please help me to correct any lies, formed when I was in my mom's womb, that affects how I identify myself. The lies being _____ (see tables below of wrong believe). Lord Jesus! Let Your truth and light replace all the lies! Reveal Your everlasting love, and Your good and pure plan which You have for my life, to my spirit in the womb. Help my spirit, soul and body be all restored back to the original form that You have created for me. Please forgive me for any rebellious self-defense mechanism that I have developed because of hurt, and for sins of rejecting life due to fear, anger and withdrawal. Renew my spirit, cleanse me, heal me and set me free.

Lord! please give me strength, courage and grace, so that I can be bold enough to face all the pain and forgive everyone who might have hurt me, especially all the pains and wounds that have been brought by my parents or close relatives, including _____ [express out every painful feeling, or issues that the Holy Spirit has revealed and surfaced in your memory, ex. Fear, shock, nervousness, unstableness, anxiety, guilt (threat to mother's life), rejection(not welcomed), shame, confusion, hatred, anger, pain, insecurity and fear of man, fear of being found(almost aborted, life being threatened)], Lord, I release all these pains and hurts, and all negative emotions to You, I let you bear these for me. Lord let Your precious blood flow through me, cleanse me, and sanctify me. Please heal every wound with the balm of Gilead, mend every broken area with Your gentle touch. Thank You Lord! For giving me a new and clean heart, remove all the defilements and wound, so I can have a righteous and wholly spirit.

In Jesus' name, I declare. My life is not a mistake, God created me with love and He has a wonderful blue print for my life. He can use everything that has happed in my life to fulfill His good will. I am created according to the will of Father God, I am created wonderfully and beautifully, I am unique, Father God knew me even before I was created (Jeremiah 1:5), and He is the one who delivered me out of my mother's womb, even though enemy tried to steal, kill and destroy me, but Father God kept me and take good care of me, and delivered my life from death. I am full of joy, and grace, I am the precious pearl on Father's palm. I renounce all the enemy's lies, my life and gender and time of

birth is not a mistake, I reject and cancel all the lies of
_____ (wrong belief in the table below) and declare
them null and void. I am beloved and blessed, I choose
to accept my life and the plan that Father God has for
me, I receive Jesus as my savior for every part of my
life, and the Holy Spirit who communicates life to me,
I pray and give thanks in Jesus' name. Amen.

Wrong Conception and Belief	Behavior often seen after Birth
I don't want to be seen	◆ Withdraw, don't want to be near people (almost being aborted), fear, phobia. Fear of life.
I am not loved	◆ Competition, performance oriented, strive for right to live, easily anger, self defense, independent. ◆ Overly self blame or self condemnation, can't say no to others, death wish, fear of developing relationship with others (want to give up own life)
I am a shameful illegitimate child	◆ Deep shameful feeling, lack of belonging, orphan, Unanchored drifting feeling (child born of wedlock), insecurity, anxiety, nervousness, fear of future.

Wrong Conception and Belief	Behavior often seen after Birth
I am a burden	◆ Dare not ask, over suppress self needs (parents facing financial or social pressure), super performer, bearing family burden, false responsibility, false guilt, self sacrifice.
I am intruder, not welcomed	◆ Not blend with parents, family members, cold relationship with others (parents not ready to get pregnant)
I have to protect mom, it's all my fault	◆ Upside down mother and son relationship, over bearing heavy burden (pregnancy cause danger to mom's health) false responsibility, self blame.

Wrong Conception and Belief	Behavior often seen after Birth
I am a mistake from beginning, I shouldn't even exist	• Gender confuse, homosexual (unexpected gender by parent) • Please parents, try to comply to parents expectation • Independent, isolation, strong will • Reject others before being rejectedI have to be good, not to cause trouble • Compromise with circumstances, self sacrifice.

Wrong Conception and Belief	Behavior often seen after Birth
I am a replacement	• Over serious, high expectations to one self, try to succeed, strive, try to repair the lost (baby conceived after previous miscarriage), anger, can't be one self.
Fear, Phobia	• Fear, lack of security, dare not give birth (Mother had difficult labor or bridge)
I am the cause of all the harm	• Nervousness, extremely sensitive, fearful, easily frightened, guilty(parents often argue or quarrel)

• Jump in immediately and control conversation or discussion whenever there is argument |

Wrong Conception and Belief	Behavior often seen after Birth
I am the cause of all the harm	• Sometimes use anger to control others • False responsibility
I have nobody to depend on, I have to depend on myself, my existence is a mistake, I came at the wrong time.	• Guilt, grief, easily self blame, easily angered, bitterness, bitter root expectation to be abandoned, death wish, fear of death, lonely, depression, frustration, abnormally desire of someone, alone, isolation, deep grief, believe no one will remember me (Mom lost father or dear ones or facing great lost during pregnancy)

Wrong Conception and Belief	Behavior often seen after Birth
Sexual intercourse is horrible	• Reject and fear of sexual intimacy, fear of man's sexual organ (Mother was raped and cause pregnant or bad sexual intimacy experience during pregnancy) • Anger
I am never full	• Hunger never satisfied, easily angry(mom over controls food intake during pregnant period, control weight or due to morning sickness)

[Release of Emotions]

Before the release of emotions, please use the "cleaning prayer after ministry", to cut soul ties with those who caused your emotion damage. Note: the soul ties you cut is the ungodly ties, normally related to negative emotion, and ungodly mind set toward emotion, it will not affect positive emotion and memories.

[Ask Lord to Help Accept one's Own Emotion]

Lord Jesus! Thank you for the emotions You created in me, so that I can feel all sorts of richness in life, Please forgive me that I have been ignoring, repressing, and shut down my emotions and memory, including: _____ (say out feelings one have ignored, such as: Lord help me to feel the negative emotions about issues and people that hurt me; such as being rejected, hurt, guilt, powerlessness, injustice, mental stress, pain, bitterness, resentment, anger, not loved, despised, depressed, suppressed, self-loathing, low self-esteem, frustration, forced to compromise, to be insulted, anxiety, confusion, restlessness, nervousness, shame, phobia, fear (fearing of loss of reputation, fear of failure, fear of being criticized, fear of being cursed, etc.). Lord, please forgive me for I have been rejecting, suppressing, and neglecting my own emotions, memories and feelings for a long time. I confess that I cannot overcome all the hurt that these feelings and memories have brought to me, but choose to reject and shut down all those memories and feelings. Please forgive me for being afraid of being hurt, I choose to defend and camouflage myself, closed my heart, refusing to feel my pain and those of others, and have allowed bitterness and unforgiveness become deeply rooted in my heart, and that has caused me to not be able to accept the loving kindness, forgiveness, and grace through salvation. Holy Spirit! Please help me, bring my emotions and memories back to my consciousness.

[Forgive those who caused our Emotional Shut Down]

Lord Jesus, I choose to forgive those who have hurt me in my youth, gave me wrong teachings, formed wrong mind sets in me and made me feel that I have no freedom to express my emotions and thoughts. I also choose to forgive those who have caused me to feel rejected and hurt, including_____, I release each and everyone of them into the freedom of my forgiveness, I release them from the debts they might owe me, especially love and freedom.

[Plead for Healing]

Lord Jesus! Please fill me with Your love and grant me grace so that I can face all my pain. Set me free from these pains, nourish me in Your love, that by Your stripes I am healed, by the chastisement upon Him I can have peace (Isaiah 53:5). Lord Jesus! I want to pour all my negative emotions out to You, I want to express all my heart and thought out to You, just like king David. Please help me release and express all these emotions to You without reservation. Help me cast down all my worries to you, for You care for me. (1 Peter 5:7). Please forgive all my iniquities, and heal all my diseases (Psalm 103:3), especially all the wounds of my spirit, soul and body which have caused negative emotions to rise up in my life. In Jesus' name I break and up root all the poison darts, arrows and roots caused by all these negative emotions, inclusive of all the bitterness, judgments, self-defenses, and inner vows. Lord, make it so that I receive the joy, peace, freedom and abundant blessings. Let my spirit, soul, body commune with You, triune God so I can be build up and made into a new creation in You.

[Accept Self and Others]

Lord Jesus, please forgive me for all the damage I have made to myself or others in the effort of trying to reduce my pain or out of self-defense, including _____ (ask Holy Spirit to reveal ungodly actions or behavior, mind set ...etc. speak out whatever comes to your mind, either memory or emotion and feeling). Holy Spirit, please help me to accept myself and everyone, who have hurt me, in God's love. Lord Jesus, I ask you to bless and heal everyone who was hurt by my emotional actions. I ask for the peace of the Holy Spirit and healing and comfort to touch and heal and fill everyone, let us all receive love and blessings that come from You.

[Praise]

O, Lord God! I praise Thee! Great and mighty, glory, strength, majesty are You. All heaven and earth belong to You. Thy is the Kingdom, You are most high, the headship of all. The LORD is my strength and song, and You are my salvation, my God (Exodus 15:2). Father God! Praise You. Your right hand, O LORD, is majestic in power, Your right hand, O LORD, shatters the enemy. (Exodus 15:6) "In Your lovingkindness You have led the people whom You have redeemed; In Your strength You have guided them to Your holy habitation. Lord! Praise You, You grant those who mourn in Zion, Giving them a garland instead of ashes, the oil of gladness instead of mourning, the mantle of praise instead of a spirit of fainting. Praise You we will be called oaks of righteousness, the planting of the LORD, that Father God may be glorified. (Isaiah 61:3) Praise You, You are the Lord who give peace, healing, comfort, goodness, and kindness, praise You, You are holy and righteous, You set the captives free. (Please continue praise the Lord, until you are filled by His joy, peace and freedom, Hallelujah!).

[Set free from Depression]

If your emotion have been suppressed for a long time, please use the prayer of release emotion. Remember to forgive those who hurt you (use the prayer of forgiveness in the break off bitter root judgment prayer), renounce all lies you have believed, especially lies related to your life, value, and destiny, use Truth to replace all lies (refer to Who am I in Christ)

This prayer only deal with emotional and spiritual problems, it will not replace medicines that prescribed by your Doctor. If you have issues in this area, please consult your Doctor, do not make decisions by yourself.

O, Lord Jesus! Please help me, set me free from all my negative emotions, give me a peaceful heart, help me cast all my worries to you, because You care for me.(1 peter 5:7) Please show me those events and reasons that are causing me to feel down. Open the eyes of my heart, so that I can face the fact and see the truth, and release all my negative emotions to You, let You truly be the Lord of my emotion. (Tell Jesus frankly about your feeling, you can start by saying "Jesus, I feel..."). In Jesus' name, I command all evil spirits related to my negative emotions to go out of me, go where Jesus sends you, never to return or disturb me. (Name all the spirit and cast them out ... spirits that cause anger, anxiety, worry, sadness, faint, sorrow, miserable,

247

insecure, jealous, depressed, bitterness, despair, lonely, fear, phobia, frighten, horrible, confused, guilt feelings, spirit of lies, and deception...etc.)

Lord Jesus! Please reveal to me about the reasons that have caused me to feel worry, grief, sad, miserable, including _____. Lord Jesus, please grant me Your wisdom and forgive me that I have sinned against You by suppressing my anger toward myself, others and also You. Forgive me that I have accepted the lies from the enemy regarding my life and hurts, that have led me to be unable to know your grace and abundant blessing, I confess the sin of hurting myself in spirit, soul and body, because I suppressed my anger and did not come before You to cast my burdens to You. Please help me to release my anger, and the fear behind my anger to You. Help me to see things from Your sight and Your thought. Shine the light of truth into my thought and mind, help me to see the Truth, that I can use Truth to interpret events, and to renounce and reject all the lies, criticisms, judgments, negative mind set, and altitude and to replace all lies with truth. I plead Your precious blood to cover and smear every area and corner of my spirit, soul and body. Hide me under the shadows of Your wings. Guard my thought and mind from all evil and lies.

O, Lord! Please give me wisdom and strength to renounce and fight against lies from the enemy. Please give me wisdom to discern my problem and environment, give me courage to change what you want me to change, help me to tolerate what I can't change. Thank You Lord, You have designed for me a unique blue print for my life, I know my life is in Your hand. Please help me to firm my step to enlarge the place of my tent, and stretch forth the curtains of my habitations; spare not: lengthen my cords, and strengthen my stakes, I put myself into Your hand and look upon You.

O, Lord! When the enemy make my spirit overwhelmed and faint within me [wrapped in gloom]; my heart within my bosom grows numb, please help me to remember the days of old; I meditate on all Your doings; I ponder the work of Your hands. Make me spread forth my hands to You; make my soul thirsts after You like a thirsty land [for water]. O, Lord! Cause me to hear Your loving-kindness in the morning, for on You do I lean and in You do I trust. Cause me to know the way wherein I should walk, for I lift up my inner self to You. Deliver me, O Lord, from my enemies; I flee to You to hide me. Teach me to do Your will, for You are my God; let Your good Spirit lead me into a level country and into the land of uprightness. Save my life, O Lord, for Your name's sake; in Your righteousness, bring my life out of trouble and free me from distress. (Psalm 143), for You are God full of mercy and grace.

O, Lord! Please help me out by revealing the truth to me,

whenever I go through trials that I can't overcome, the troubled emotions caused by the enemies; when I can't come before You to pour my heart out, and am unable to control my emotions before others, or when I enter into a negative mind set (or thinking patterns), please remind me that You have prepared for me abundant blessings, help me know I am blessed and beloved, and help me to know who am I in Christ. Help me to endure through steadfastness and patience for then I shall win the true life of my soul.(Luke 21:19). Reveal to me Your riches love and grace and Your wisdom, help me to see Your blessing and goodness even in my dilemma. Help me to agree with Your will and plan, and reject the lies of enemy. O, Lord! Please refresh and restore my life; and leads me into the paths of righteousness for Your name's sake. Yes, help me even though I walk through the [deep, sunless] valley of the shadow of death, I will fear or dread no evil, for You are with me; Your rod [to protect] and Your staff [to guide], they comfort me. You prepare a table before me in the presence of my enemies. You anoint my head with oil; my [brimming] cup runs over (Psalm 23).

O, Lord! "A cheerful heart is a good medicine; but a broken spirit dries up the bones."(prov.17:22); "A glad heart makes a cheerful countenance, but by sorrow of heart the spirit is broken."(prov.15:13). Lord, please anoint me with the Spirit of Joy, to replace the spirit of sorrow, help me to receive the joy and peace that comes from You. For the joy of the Lord is our strength and stronghold." (Nehemiah 8:10). Let everlasting joy be upon our heads; we shall obtain joy and gladness, and sorrow and sighing shall flee away. (Isaiah 35:10) For You will be moved to compassion according to the multitude of Your loving-kindness and tender mercy. (Lamentation 3:32) For You do not willingly and from Your heart afflict or grieve us, or to trample and crush underfoot all the prisoners of the earth. Thank You Lord, for You are the Lord who loves me, I pray in gratitude, in Jesus' name. Amen.

[Prayer for Deliverance from Fear]

Abba Father! Thank You for You are God who loves me, You love me without any condition. You know me before I came into this world, Your eyes saw my unformed body; all the days ordained for me were written in your book before one of them came to be, and You are the One who cause me out of my mother's womb. You saw all the days of my life; I went through fire, through water, through river, through hardship, You know all. You know when I go through fear, I experience terror. Thank you for keeping me well until today with Your might and grace. You sent Your only begotten son Jesus Christ to die for me on the cross, even while I was still dead in my transgression and iniquities, You have shown me how deep, wide, long and high is Your great love and mercy. You drew me with Your love to enter into the Kingdom of Your beloved Son, to be redeemed and forgiven from all my transgressions. So I can draw near with confidence to the throne of grace, so that I may receive mercy and find grace to help me in a time of need. Your word teaches me, I shall lean on You, whenever I am afraid. Your perfect love cast out all fear. If You are for me, who can be against me!

Lord Jesus, I confess that I still cannot overcome the emotion of fear inside of me, please help me. I submit every fearful part of my spirit and soul into your hand, I ask You, arise in me and sit on the throne of every part of my life. Pour Your unconditional and unlimited Love in me, fill me, saturate me, wrap every wounded part, fearful part, or the part have experienced terror with Your gentle love and comfort them. Let Your shalom (peace) fill them and surround them, hide them under the shadow of Your wings, lead them to the green pastures and lay them beside the still water, let them find rest in Your arm, cover them with Your precious blood so that no enemy can find them until the day they can be fully healed. I cast all my fear, anxiety, nervousness, worry and all the negative emotions and thoughts into Your hand. You are my light and my redeemer, whom shall I fear? I will depend on You, whenever I am afraid, You lift my head, and my head will be lifted up above my enemies who around me, I will not shake for I depend on You, You are my rock, my fortress and my refuge. Still my lips shall praise You! Your loving kindness, O LORD, extends to the heavens, Your faithfulness *reaches* to the skies. You are worthy to be praised, worthy to receive all glory and honor. Amen

[Overcome witchcraft Prayer]

(The actual use of magic, witchcraft way to curse people are not included in here)

Note: Pray and ask the Holy Spirit revealing to you whether you are impacted by any witchcraft power, and the person who is practicing witchcraft that affects you; or to reveal oneself any need to correct the behavior of witchcraft, the following methods are reference only, it cannot replace personal revelation that come from the Holy Spirit.

1.   Definition of witchcraft: the idea and/or prophecies of a person who imposes these on others, contrary to human free will and life, is witchcraft.

2.   Operating behavior of a person who use witchcraft: Using method with crying, stress, emotional stress and other emotional ties bind or intimidate, threats to give pressure to others through domination, manipulation, control, influencing others to achieve an objective.

3.   Behaviors of those who are affected by witchcraft: ideological confusion, unable to make decisions, and will seek recognition again and again from the controller, and cannot freely express their ideas and opinions, and have a sense of unknown

hatred and anger, cannot make decisions and feel rejected, isolated, lonely, frustrated, depressed, loss of vision and future direction, feelings of guilt, loss of joy, no vitality.

4.	The order of severity of those being affected by witchcraft: loose heart, confusion, depression and guilt, loss of vision and future direction, withdraw and do not want to get back and disappointment and despair, feel they have been defeated by enemies and give up control of their own ideas and perseverance.

[Those who are affected by witchcraft]

(First cut off soul ties with "cleansing prayer", to forgive those who use of witchcraft or who use control. If one subjected to negative attacks, threatening words, then you should use "the prayer of break off wrong judgments and curses" to forgive then break soul ties.)

In the name of Jesus Christ, I cut all the links between _____ (name) who control the unclean spirit and all evil spirits that come from the magic and sorcerers and all the spirit, soul and body links between me and _____ (name) . In the name of Jesus Christ, I command and reject all the evil spirit that caused me to have symptoms of headaches, back pain, systemic pain and heaviness, frustration, loose heart, discouraged, confusion, depression and guilt, disappointment, despair, depression, defeated, control, chaos, grief to leave me, go out to where Jesus Christ want you to go, never to return, you no longer affect me. Father God, Please send an army of angels to camp and guard all around me, and cover me with the blood of Jesus Christ from my head to toe, every area and part of me. In Jesus' name I break off all powers of control and domination, especially the control and repression that come from the human authority. Lord, please also show me the root source of all these problems including the unknown sense of hatred and anger, inability to make decisions, feel rejected, isolated, lonely, depressed, no foresight, guilt, loss of joy, no vitality, loss of vision and the lost of future direction, withdrawn, disappointment and despair, defeated, being controlled, giving up my own ideas.

Lord please awaken my spirit and soul so that I can clearly receive word and abundance from God. I cancel all the attacks of words, thoughts, ideas, behaviors, control and curses from all the evil spirits. The Lord did not give me a spirit of timidity but a spirit of power, love, and sound mind. I am not afraid of all the words, thoughts, behavior, and control that come from people. I only fear the Lord God, and focus on Your will and the destiny You have set for my life.

O, Lord! Please help me, let my heart be quiet and my soul wait in silence   for Thee alone. For only Thou art my rock and my salvation, my Defense and my Fortress. I shall not be greatly moved. (Psalm 62:1-2). In the name of Jesus Christ, I cancel all personal and spiritual attacks, threats, destruction, corruption, falseness, bullying, adding insult to injury, robbery, lie, smear, deceit, curse, all the tricks and hurts. In the name of Jesus Christ I declare them null and void, they no longer have any effect or spiritual significance. O, Lord! Let all naught vanish, all the corruption perish, so they no longer disturb or hurt me. O, Lord! Please forgive and bless everyone who have hurt, annoyed, or attacked me in the process. Lord! Break all ungodly spirit, soul and body links between them and Jezebel, witchcraft, sorcerers, control spirits. Help them and set them free so that they too can recognize and enjoy the joy of Thy salvation. O, Lord! Arise and scatter thy enemies. You are victorious because of my forgiveness and blessings; I shall receive double blessings instead of the abuse and sham. O, Lord! Let Your river of living water pour greatly into our lives and our environment. Let Thy righteousness be my breastplate and Your oil of joy be upon me instead of sorrow, because of Thy help, my head is held high over the enemies which surround me, for You are my light and my salvation.

O, Lord! Please forgive and help all those who have done deceit and witchcraft, because they do not know what they have done. Please have mercy and grace over them, enlighten their heart, reveal problems, help them learn of repentance, to know your salvation in the process and know the hope and blessing of Your calling. O, Lord! Please draw them closer to You, to have intimate relationship with You, and to love You deeper. They can be deeply rooted in Thy love, securely founded on the rock of Thy love, let Thy love be poured deep into their hearts, so they all become the vessel and pipes of Thy love, to demonstrate Thy glory. The Lord will grant [consolation and joy] to those who mourn in Zion-to give them an ornament (a garland or diadem) of beauty instead of ashes, the oil of joy instead of mourning, the garment [expressive] of praise instead of a heavy, burdened, and failing spirit-that we may be called oaks of righteousness [lofty, strong, and magnificent, distinguished for uprightness, justice, and right standing with God], the planting of the Lord, that He may be glorified. (Isaiah 61:3). Lord! Please give wisdom and words from heaven, "A joyful heart is good medicine, but a broken spirit dries up the bones (Proverbs 17:22)," Lord, make much of heavenly joy fill me, permeate me, cleanse me, and heal me. Break off all the chaos and disturbance; let Thy oil of joy anoint me like water. O, Lord! Help my soul rest in peace and be quiet in Thee. Let every part of me can be completely filled by Thy joy! Lord! I praise Thee! Lord! Thou art omniscient, omnipotent and omnipresent God! O, Lord! I praise Thee! I praise Thee! Let me truly understand and know the will of Father God. Abba Father! Thank You for filling my soul and every part of my body with the oil of joy. Thank You for saturating every corner of my family, work, ministry. Cast out all the stealing, killing and destruction that come from the enemy. O, Lord! I thank thee! Thy joy is the source of my strength, thank You! Thy grace is the source of my blessings, I thank You and praise Thee as the source of all my joy and blessing.

O, Lord! I praise You for You are Almighty God, my Salvation, my rock, my fortress, and my refuge, I love You with all my heart forever more.

[Repent from Using Witchcraft]

Lord, Please reveal to me and forgive me what I have done to others by using various languages, behavior, attitudes, relationships with the people around me to control and manipulate them because of _____ and various other reasons. I confess this is the sin of witchcraft and sorcery. Please forgive me that I have _____(express out people and things that are floating in thought at this moment, for example: Lord, Please forgive me for the sins that where I used man's method over God's method on multiple occasions. Please forgive me for the sins that on many times that I thought I was caring for others, using my own thoughts and beliefs to persuade and pressure others to agree with me and do the things I think is good for them. Lord, Please forgive me for the sins that although I think of love as a starting point, but applied a variety of arguments, means, rumors, partial facts, exaggeration, taking things out of context, intimidation, threats, pressure, and pretended to be pitiful to gain sympathy to achieve what I want to achieve.) I confess I have sinned against You, I repent and turn away from my sinful behavior. Lord help me not to employ the ways of human work, but wish to seek thy will and thy ways, to deal with things around me with the fruit of the Spirit, love, joy, patience, peace, kindness, goodness, faithfulness, gentleness and self-control. Lord, please help me learn to know God's ways and use those ways to deal with things. Holy Spirit please lead me and keep me in the learning process, so that I will no longer make the same mistake, so that I may glorify God and benefit Your people. I bless everyone that I have hurt before, Lord, let Thy grace, love, and healing power be released unto them, so that they can be healed completely. I pray with thanksgiving and appreciation in the name of Jesus Christ. Amen.

[Renounce Religious spirit]

Description:

1.   Definition: Religious spirit embedded in the Church, tries to use religious activities to replace the desire to know God in human's heart, it is very difficult to be detected. Definition by Peter Wagner: *"the spirit of religion is an agent of Satan assigned to prevent change and to maintain the status quo by using religious devices"* Jonas Clark: *"The religious spirit is a dark power that make people perform religious, self-righteousness or super spiritual. The main purpose of this spirit is to block God's people to know Jesus, to hinder God's work of building His glorious Church."*

2.   Symptoms of religious spirit: see attached

3.   Operating strategies: It cause people to believe that they can find strength or ways to be saved or receive blessings without God. It causes people to believe that God is not almighty, He will not fulfill His promise, will not complete His command, God will not do what He says.

Lord Jesus! Please forgive me for all ungodly belief systems that I have developed due to wrong teaching, hurt or blindness, I confess that I did not behold upon You, and allowed religious value and beliefs(the

261

leavens of Pharisees and Sadducees) to affect me. I
confess that I had believed _____ (speak out loud
all the ungodly belief system, see attached), I repent
of every sin that I have committed due to wrong
belief system, I need to be delivered from the spirit
of religion. Lord, please be the Lord of all my values,
belief and behavior.

Holy Spirit, come! Pour, pour into me, fill me. I renounce
all these wrong beliefs, I cancel all the agreement I
have made with all these lies, and replace them with
truth. Holy Spirit, help me to come out from all these
wrong beliefs and let truth to be implanted deeply in
my heart. In Jesus' name, I command all the spirit of
religion and all other related spirit to leave me, go out
to where Jesus wants you to go, never to come back or
disturb anyone else.

*Lord, please help me to love the Lord God with all my
heart, all my mind, and all my strength. Help me to
honor You as my priority. Help me not to live under
laws and regulations, renounce perfectionism, criticism,
judgments, control, self-righteousness, rebellious,
gangs, help me to break all wrong believes and change
my behavioral pattern. In Jesus name, I declare that I
reject all philosophy and empty deception, the tradition
of men, and the elementary principles of the world to
replace the truth of the Christ. (Colossian 2:8) Please
help me to stay fresh in You always, and help me not to*

be conformed to this world, but be transformed by the renewing of my mind, so that I may be able to prove what the will of God is, that which is good and acceptable and perfect.(Roman 12:2) Make me see others through Your eyes, to love and tolerate with Your loving kindness, to see other's strength, not weaknesses.

Lord, help me to keep my mouth, my heart more than anything else. Pride goes before destruction, and a haughty spirit before stumbling. (Proverb 16:18). Help me to realize the arrogance, self-defense, self-righteousness, complaints, criticisms, slander, selfishness, nonteachability, irresponsibility, hypocrisy, and false humility. Help me transform my mind and behavior, so that I can have Your heart as my heart, to love my neighbors, not lift myself up, but truly let go of all my pride and reputation, to love You with all my heart and lift Your name on high.

Lord, help me not to blame You on the things which happened in my life or my environment, make me truly know Your will, and learn the lessons of life. Help me to see the truth that You want me to see, and grow in wisdom and help me to know You more. Help me to take the responsibilities that I need to take, keep me far away from bitterness and accusation. Lord, help me know my identity as the son of the living God, You already given me the authority and weapons for spiritual battle, give me Your strategies to help me, and remind me to

263

put on the full armor You have given me, so that I can resist the day of evil, having done everything, to stand firm. (Eph. 6:13) Help me to reject and renounce all the influences from the tree of knowledge of good and evil, and live in the grace of tree of life. Help me not to serve You with my own strength, or my own intellect and wisdom. Thank You for giving me grace, peace, joy, strength, faithfulness, boldness, thank You for became poor for us, so that we can be rich (2 Cor. 8:9). Help us to stand firm in this generation, to resist, fight, persevere, continuously pursue God, to be delivered, healed, continuously believe in salvation, hoping for God's promise and everlasting blessings.

In Jesus name, I proclaim I am son/daughter of the Living God, God has a special divine plan and destiny for me. Lord, I praise You and thank You for the blessings and grace You have given to me. I confess and repent for all the sins I have been involved in or agreed with that related to religious myth, fear, rituals , tradition, pride, legalism, judgment, control, hypocrisy, blame towards God, resentment, anger with God, isolation with man and God, grief, and living in the tree of knowledge. I also choose to forgive everyone who have influenced me in all these believes and behaviors, I release each and every one of them into the freedom of my forgiveness. In Jesus name, I break all the ungodly spirit, soul and body links in between me and everyone I have forgiven and all the sins and ungodly beliefs.

Thank You Lord, for You bring my sin as far as the east is from the west. In Jesus name, I declare all the spirit of religion and all the cohorts (pride, control, witchcraft, disappointment, and bitterness ...etc.), has no more right over me, I command you to go where Jesus wants you to go, never to disturb me. In Jesus victorious name. Amen.

Character	Description
Focus on Tree of knowledge Despise Tree of Life	◆ Only focus on knowledge, skill, research of bible, scripture, focus on right or wrong, make people try to know God through knowledge and understanding and not seek for the help of Holy Spirit ◆ Pursue devotion and spiritual conference instead of having personal relationship with God.
Ritualism (Insistence of tradition)	◆ Prayer, devotion and ministry by method and program. (Focus on ministry instead of Jesus, ex. Eli, 1 Sam. 3:13-14). In failure one will start feeling guilt and fall into fear and self accusation ◆ Only glorify what God has done in the past but reject His new movement.

Character	Description
Ritualism (Insistence of tradition)	◆ Prideful attitude and assume one already knows God's opinion, and reject unknown spiritual phenomenon. ◆ Doubt or against new things/ actions, especially when the action did not follow old habits. This is the beginning of jealousy and pride, believing God will not use others to do new things, only what we have is the best.
Deny Truth	◆ Deny God's word and character, lift up hypocrite and distort truth. ◆ Can't receive any grace without own effort. This is the bitterroot of religious spirit. Have to depend on own strife and feel guilty because of failing God's standard.

Character	Description
Jealousy	• Rise against God's prophet (eg. Gain), imitate God's expression. (mainly in church), attack pastors or bishop because of jealousy and competition.
	• Self-centered ministry, feel good and happy when own result is better than others, otherwise feel depressed
	• Over react to other member's immature and fleshly behavior and ignore other people's improvement
Destroys Relationship	• The main purpose of religious spirit is to destroy things that it thinks is not right. There is more destruction and dividing work in his life and ministry than that to building and growing.

Character	Description
Destroys Relationship	• Destroying human relationship: Backbiters, criticism; judgment, self-righteousness, betrayal, creating factions
	• Shut people up through rejection and false testimony.
	• Destroy relationship with people, refuse to reconcile and isolate from other saints.
	• Destroy relationship with God.
	• Steal joy, compassion towards God,
	• Loose hope, dream, vision and calling.
	• Believe that God will not speak to me, feel that "I have already lost the authority of the son of God, given up spiritual gift and to slumber".

Character	Description
Spiritual Pride	• Refuse any correction from others, especially when it comes from people that "we believe who are spiritually less matured then us." • Insist to only listen to God not any man, says: no one is better than me, no one can be my spiritual teacher. • Feeling I am closer to the Lord than others, my ministry or life is better than others. • Elder son syndrome: Prideful by following the law, compare self with others but without God's "mercy and grace". (1 Cor. 10:12). • Self-righteousness, thinks of self being higher than others.

Character	Description
Spiritual Pride	◆ Feel offended or shamed because people reject the title or ministries that have been proclaimed.
Hypocrites	◆ Legalistic, criticizing, judging, bias, thinking that self is closer to God, seemingly rich in the spirit but actually poor and self righteous ◆ Seeing other's weaknesses more than strengths, and using this to gain for one's own benefit in ministry. ◆ Self-appointed prophet and believes self to be send by God to show the way and correct others. Criticize people with no love and mercy, most of time cause more disturbances. Creates chaos and division.

Character	Description
Hypocrites	◆ Self-appointed prophet and believes self to be send by God to show the way and correct others. Criticize people with no love and mercy, most of time cause more disturbances. Creates chaos and division. ◆ Perform to get attention and praise, become angry, feelings of insignificance if being neglected, fear of man (idol) more than God. ◆ Think of self glory more than God's glory. ◆ Having a form of godliness, but corrupt inside, behave good in front of people, wearing masks (fake identity), inconsistent, changeable, covers mistakes, dishonest.

Character	Description
Mercilessness	• Strict, no grace and mercy to others • Domineering, imperious and impatient to others' weaknesses and failures. • Over react to other's emotional behavior, criticize or rebukes when people needs grace and mercy..

(Reference: Characters of religious spirit by Rick Joyner, and Conquering the religious spirit by pastor Tommy Femrite)

[Because God Loves Me]

✿   Because God loves me, He is slow to lose patience with me.

✿   Because God loves me, He does not treat me as an object to be possessed and manipulated.

✿   Because God loves me, He has no need to impress me with how great and powerful He is because He is God; nor does He belittle me as His child in order to show me how important He is.

✿   Because God loves me, He is for me. He wants to see me mature and develop in His love.

✿   Because God loves me, He does not send down His wrath on every little mistake I make, of which they are many.

✿   Because God loves me, He does not keep score of all my sins and then beat me over the head with them whenever He gets the chance.

✿   Because God loves me, He is deeply grieved when I do not walk in the ways that please Him because He sees this as evidence that I don't trust

Him and love Him as I should.

✿   Because God loves me, He rejoices when I experience His power and strength and stand up under the pressures of life for His Name's sake.

✿   Because God loves me, He keeps on working patiently with me even when I feel like giving up and can't see why He doesn't give up on me, too.

✿   Because God loves me, He keeps on trusting me when at times I don't even trust myself.

✿   Because God loves me, He never says there is no hope for me. Rather, He patiently works with me and disciplines me in such a way that it is hard for me to understand the depth of His concern for me.

✿   Because God loves me, He never forsakes me even though many of my friends might.

✿   Because God loves me, He stands with me when I have reached the rock bottom of despair, when I see the real me and compare that with His righteousness, holiness, beauty and love. It is at a moment like this that I can really believe that God loves me.

[Father's Love Letter]

My Child ~
You may not know me, but I know everything about you ~ *Psalm 139:1*
I know when you sit down and when you rise up ~ *Psalm 139:2*
I am familiar with all your ways ~ *Psalm 139:3*
Even the very hairs on your head are numbered ~ *Matthew 10:29-31*
For you were made in my image ~ *Genesis 1:27*
In me you live and move and have your being ~ *Acts 17:28*
For you are my offspring ~ *Acts 17:28*
I knew you even before you were conceived ~ *Jeremiah 1:4-5*
I chose you when I planned creation ~ *Ephesians 1:11-12*
You were not a mistake, for all your days are written in my book ~ *Psalm 139:15-16*
I determined the exact time of your birth and where you would live ~ *Acts 17:26*
You are fearfully and wonderfully made ~ *Psalm 139:14*
I knit you together in your mother's womb ~ *Psalm 139:13*
And brought you forth on the day you were born ~ *Psalm 71:6*
I have been misrepresented by those who don't

know me ~ *John 8:41-44*

I am not distant and angry, but am the complete expression of love ~ *1 John 4:16*

And it is my desire to lavish my love on you ~ *1 John 3:1*

Simply because you are my child and I am your father ~ *1 John 3:1*

I offer you more than your earthly father ever could ~ *Matthew 7:11* For I am the perfect father ~ *Matthew 5:48*

Every good gift that you receive comes from my hand ~ *James 1:17*

For I am your provider and I meet all your needs ~ *Matthew 6:31-33*

My plan for your future has always been filled with hope ~ *Jeremiah 29:11*

Because I love you with an everlasting love ~ *Jeremiah 31:3*

My thoughts toward you are countless as the sand on the seashore ~ *Psalm 139:17-18*

And I rejoice over you with singing ~ *Zephaniah 3:17*

I will never stop doing good to you ~ *Jeremiah 32:40*

For you are my treasured possession ~ *Exodus 19:5*

I desire to establish you with all my heart and all my soul ~ *Jeremiah 32:41*

And I want to show you great and marvelous things ~ *Jeremiah 33:3*

If you seek me with all your heart, you will find me ~ *Deuteronomy 4:29* Delight in me and I will give you the desires of your heart ~ *Psalm 37:4* For it is I who gave you those desires ~ *Philippians 2:13*

I am able to do more for you than you could possibly imagine ~ *Ephesians 3:20*

For I am your greatest encourager ~ *2 Thessalonians 2:16-17*

I am also the Father who comforts you in all your troubles ~ *2 Corinthians 1:3-4*

When you are brokenhearted, I am close to you ~ *Psalm 34:18*

As a shepherd carries a lamb, I have carried you close to my heart ~ *Isaiah 40:11*

One day I will wipe away every tear from your eyes ~ *Revelation 21:3-4*

And I'll take away all the pain you have suffered on this earth ~ *Revelation 21:3-4*

I am your Father, and I love you even as I love my son, Jesus ~ *John 17:23*

For in Jesus, my love for you is revealed ~ *John 17:26*

He is the exact representation of my being ~ *Hebrews 1:3*

He came to demonstrate that I am for you, not against you ~ *Romans 8:31*

And to tell you that I am not counting your sins ~
2 Corinthians 5:18-19
Jesus died so that you and I could be reconciled ~
2 Corinthians 5:18-19
 His death was the ultimate expression of my
love for you ~ *1 John 4:10*
I gave up everything I loved that I might gain your
love ~ *Romans 8:31-32*
If you receive the gift of my son Jesus, you
receive me ~ *1 John 2:23*
And nothing will ever separate you from my love
again ~ Romans 8:38-39
Come home and I'll throw the biggest party
heaven has ever seen ~ *Luke 15:7*
I have always been Father, and will always be
Father ~ Ephesians 3:14-15
My question is ~ Will you be my child? ~
John 1:12-13
I am waiting for you ~ Luke 15:11-32

Love,
Your Dad, Almighty God

Origin from http://www.fathersloveletter.com

[Who I am in Christ]

1. I am able
Philippians 4:13— I can do all things through Christ who strengthens me.

2. I am abounding in grace
2 Cor. 9:8— And God is able to make all grace abound toward you, that you, always having all sufficiency in all things, may have an abundance for every good work.

3. I am abounding in hope
Rom. 15:4— For whatever things were written before were written for our learning, that we through the patience and comfort of the Scriptures might have hope. Rom. 15:13Now may the God of hope fill you with all joy and peace in believing, that you may abound in hope by the power of the Holy Spirit.

4. I am Abraham's offspring
Gal. 3:29—So then those who are of faith are blessed with believing Abraham.

5. I am abundant
John 10:10— The thief does not come except to steal, and to kill, and to destroy. I have come that they may have life, and that they may have it

more abundantly.

6. I am accepted
Eph. 1:6— to the praise of the glory of His grace, by which He made us accepted in the Beloved.

7. I have access
Eph. 2:18— For through Him we both have access by one Spirit to the Father.

8. I am adequate
2 Cor. 3:5— Not that we are sufficient of ourselves to think of anything as being from ourselves, but our sufficiency is from God,

9. I am adopted
Eph. 1:5— having predestined us to adoption as sons by Jesus Christ to Himself, according to the good pleasure of His will,

10. I am alive
Eph.2:4-5— But God, who is rich in mercy, because of His great love with which He loved us, 5 even when we were dead in trespasses, made us alive together with Christ (by grace you have been saved),

11. I am an ambassador for Christ
2 Cor. 5:20— Now then, we are ambassadors for

Christ, as though God were pleading through us: we implore you on Christ's behalf, be reconciled to God.

12. I am anointed

1 John 2:20—But you have an anointing from the Holy One, and you know all things

13. I am anxious for nothing

Phil. 4:6—Be anxious for nothing, but in everything by prayer and supplication, with thanksgiving, let your requests be made known to God

14. I am the apple of His eye

Zechariah 2:8—For thus says the LORD of hosts: "He sent Me after glory, to the nations which plunder you; for he who touches you touches the apple of His eye.

15. I am appointed by God

John 15:16—You did not choose Me, but I chose you and appointed you that you should go and bear fruit, and that your fruit should remain, that whatever you ask the Father in My name He may give you.

16. I am the fragrance of Christ

2 Cor. 2:15—For we are to God the fragrance of

Christ among those who are being saved and among those who are perishing.

17. I am not ashamed

2 Timothy 1:12—For this reason I also suffer these things; nevertheless I am not ashamed, for I know whom I have believed and am persuaded that He is able to keep what I have committed to Him until that Day.

18. I am assured of reward

1 Cor. 15:58 Therefore, my beloved brethren, be steadfast, immovable, always abounding in the work of the Lord, knowing that your labor is not in vain in the Lord.

19. I am assured of success

Prov. 16:3 Commit your works to the LORD, And your thoughts will be established.

20. I have authority over the devil

Luke 9:1 Then He called His twelve disciples together and gave them power and authority over all demons, and to cure diseases.

21. I am baptized into Christ

1 Cor. 12:13 For by one Spirit we were all baptized into one body—whether Jews or Greeks, whether slaves or free—and have all been made

to drink into[c] one Spirit.

22. I am beautiful
Psalm 149:4—For the LORD takes pleasure in His people. He will beautify the humble with salvation.

23. I am becoming a mature person
Eph. 4:13—till we all come to the unity of the faith and of the knowledge of the Son of God, to a perfect man, to the measure of the stature of the fullness of Christ;

24. I am becoming conformed to Christ
Romans 8:29—For whom He foreknew, He also predestined to be conformed to the image of His Son, that He might be the firstborn among many brethren.

25. I am a believer
Rom. 10:9—that if you confess with your mouth the Lord Jesus and believe in your heart that God has raised Him from the dead, you will be saved.

26. I belong to God
John 17:9—I pray for them. I do not pray for the world but for those whom You have given Me, for they are Yours.

27. I am betrothed

Hosea 2:19-20 19—" I will betroth you to Me forever. Yes, I will betroth you to Me In righteousness and justice, In lovingkindness and mercy; 20 I will betroth you to Me in faithfulness, And you shall know the LORD.

28. I am blameless
1 Cor. 1:8—who will also confirm you to the end, that you may be blameless in the day of our Lord Jesus Christ.

29. I am blessed
Eph. 1:3—Blessed be the God and Father of our Lord Jesus Christ who has blessed us with every spiritual blessing in the heavenly places in Christ.

30. I am blood bought
1 Cor. 6:19-20—Or do you not know that your body is the temple of the Holy Spirit who is in you, whom you have from God, and you are not your own? 20 For you were bought at a price; therefore glorify God in your body[c] and in your spirit, which are God's.

31. I am bold
Prov. 28:1—The wicked flee when no one pursues. But the righteous are bold as a lion.

32. I am a bond servant
Psalm 116:16—O LORD, truly I am Your
servant; I am Your servant, the son of Your
maidservant; You have loosed my bonds.

33. I am born of God
1 John 5:18—Therefore the Jews sought all the
more to kill Him, because He not only broke the
Sabbath, but also said that God was His Father,
making Himself equal with God.

34. I am born again
1 Peter 1:23—having been born again, not of
corruptible seed but incorruptible, through the
word of God which lives and abides forever,

35. I am bought with a price
1 Cor. 6:20—For you were bought at a price;
therefore glorify God in your body[c] and in your
spirit, which are God's.

36. I am branch of the True Vine
John 15:5—I am the vine, you are the branches.
He who abides in Me, and I in him, bears much
fruit; for without Me you can do nothing.

37. I am His Bride
Isaiah 54:5—For your Maker is your husband,
The LORD of hosts is His name; And your

Redeemer is the Holy One of Israel; He is called the God of the whole earth.

38. I am His brother
Hebrews 2:11—For both He who sanctifies and those who are being sanctified are all of one, for which reason He is not ashamed to call them brethren,

39. I am brought near
Eph. 2:13—But now in Christ Jesus you who once were far off have been brought near by the blood of Christ.

40. I am built up
1 Peter 2:5—you also, as living stones, are being built up a spiritual house, a holy priesthood, to offer up spiritual sacrifices acceptable to God through Jesus Christ.

41. I am buried with Christ
Rom.6:4—Therefore we were buried with Him through baptism into death, that just as Christ was raised from the dead by the glory of the Father, even so we also should walk in newness of life.

42. I am called
1 Peter 5:10—But may the God of all grace,

who called us to His eternal glory by Christ Jesus, after you have suffered a while, perfect, establish, strengthen, and settle you

43. I am calm
Phil 4:6—Be anxious for nothing, but in everything by prayer and supplication, with thanksgiving, let your requests be made known to God;

44. I am cared for
1 Peter 5:7—Casting all your care upon Him, for He cares for you.

45. I am carried
Exodus 19:4—'You have seen what I did to the Egyptians, and how I bore you on eagles' wings and brought you to Myself

46. I am changed
1 Samuel 10:6—Then the Spirit of the LORD will come upon you, and you will prophesy with them and be turned into another man.

47. I am a child of God
John 1:12—But as many as received Him, to them He gave the right to become children of God, to those who believe in His name

48. I am cherished
Eph. 5:29—For no one ever hated his own flesh, but nourishes and cherishes it, just as the Lord does the church.

49. I am chosen
1 Peter 2:9—But you are a chosen generation, a royal priesthood, a holy nation, His own special people, that you may proclaim the praises of Him who called you out of darkness into His marvelous light;

50. I am circumcised spiritually
Colossians 2:11—In Him you were also circumcised with the circumcision made without hands, by putting off the body of the sins[c] of the flesh, by the circumcision of Christ,

51. I am a citizen of heaven
Phil 3:20—For our citizenship is in heaven, from which we also eagerly wait for the Savior, the Lord Jesus Chris

52. I am clay in the potter's hand
Jeremiah 18:6—"O house of Israel, can I not do with you as this potter?" says the LORD. "Look, as the clay is in the potter's hand, so are you in My hand, O house of Israel!

53. I am clean

Ezekiel 36:25:—Then I will sprinkle clean water on you, and you shall be clean; I will cleanse you from all your filthiness and from all your idols
John 15:3—You are already clean because of the word which I have spoken to you.

54. I am cleansed

1 John 1:7,9—But if we walk in the light as He is in the light, we have fellowship with one another, and the blood of Jesus Christ His Son cleanses us from all sin. [9] If we confess our sins, He is faithful and just to forgive us our sins and to cleanse us from all unrighteousness.

55. I am clothed with Christ

Galatians 3:27—For as many of you as were baptized into Christ have put on Christ.

56. I am a co-heir with Christ

Romans 8:17—and if children, then heirs—heirs of God and joint heirs with Christ, if indeed we suffer with Him, that we may also be glorified together.

57. I am comforted

Jeremiah 31:13—" Then shall the virgin rejoice in the dance, And the young men and the old, together; For I will turn their mourning to joy, Will comfort them, And make them rejoice rather than sorrow.

58. I am complete in Christ
Colossians 2:10—and you are complete in Him, who is the head of all principality and power.

59. I am confident
1 John 4:17—Love has been perfected among us in this: that we may have boldness in the day of judgment; because as He is, so are we in this world.

60. I am confident of answers to prayer
1 John 5:14-15—Now this is the confidence that we have in Him, that if we ask anything according to His will, He hears us. [15] And if we know that He hears us, whatever we ask, we know that we have the petitions that we have asked of Him.

61. I am confident He will finish me
Philippians 1:6—being confident of this very thing, that He who has begun a good work in you will complete it until the day of Jesus Christ;

62. I am confident He will never leave me
Hebrews 13:5-6—Let your conduct be without covetousness; be content with such things as you have. For He Himself has said, "I will never leave

you nor forsake you." 6 So we may boldly say:

> " *The LORD is my helper;*
> *I will not fear.*
> *What can man do to me?"*

63. I am a conqueror
Romans 8:37—Yet in all these things we are more than conquerors through Him who loved us.

64. I am content
Philippians 4:11—Not that I speak in regard to need, for I have learned in whatever state I am, to be content:

65. I am content with weakness
2 Corinthians 12:10—Therefore I take pleasure in infirmities, in reproaches, in needs, in persecutions, in distresses, for Christ's sake. For when I am weak, then I am strong.

66. I am continually with God
Psalm 73:23—Nevertheless I am continually with You; You hold me by my right hand.

67. I am controlled by the love of Christ
2 Corinthians 5:14—For the love of Christ compels us, because we judge thus: that if One died for all, then all died;

68. I am courageous

1 Chronicles 28:20—And David said to his son Solomon, "Be strong and of good courage, and do it; do not fear nor be dismayed, for the LORD God—my God—will be with you. He will not leave you nor forsake you, until you have finished all the work for the service of the house of the LORD.

69. I am created in Christ for good works

Ephesians 2:10—For we are His workmanship, created in Christ Jesus for good works, which God prepared beforehand that we should walk in them.

70. I am created in His image

Genesis 1:27—So God created man in His own image; in the image of God He created him; male and female He created them.

71. I am crucified with Him

Galatians 2:20—I have been crucified with Christ; it is no longer I who live, but Christ lives in me; and the life which I now live in the flesh I live by faith in the Son of God, who loved me and gave Himself for me.

72. I am dead in Christ

Romans 6:4—Therefore we were buried with Him through baptism into death, that just as Christ was raised from the dead by the glory of the

Father, even so we also should walk in newness of life.

73. I am dead to sin
Romans 6:11—Likewise you also, reckon yourselves to be dead indeed to sin, but alive to God in Christ Jesus our Lord.

74. I am a delight
Psalm 147:11—The LORD takes pleasure in those who fear Him, In those who hope in His mercy

75. I am delighted in
Isaiah 42:1—"Behold! My Servant *whom* I uphold,

>My Elect One in whom My soul delights!
>I have put My Spirit upon Him;
>He will bring forth justice to the Gentiles.

76. I am delivered
Psalm 107:6—Then they cried out to the LORD in their trouble, and He delivered them out of their distresses.

77. I am desired
Psalm 45:11—So the King will greatly desire your beauty; Because He is your Lord, worship Him.

78. I am determined

1 Corinthians 2:2—For I determined not to know anything among you except Jesus Christ and Him crucified.

79. I am a disciple
John 8:31-32—Then Jesus said to those Jews who believed Him, "If you abide in My word, you are My disciples indeed. 32 And you shall know the truth, and the truth shall make you free."

80. I am disciplined
Hebrews 12:5-11[5]—And you have forgotten the exhortation which speaks to you as to sons:

" *My son, do not despise the chastening of the LORD,*

Nor be discouraged when you are rebuked by Him;

[6]*For whom the LORD loves He chastens,*

And scourges every son whom He receives."

[7] If you endure chastening, God deals with you as with sons; for what son is there whom a father does not chasten? [8]But if you are without chastening, of which all have become partakers, then you are illegitimate and not sons. [9]Furthermore, we have had human fathers who corrected us, and we paid them respect. Shall we not much more readily be in subjection to the Father of spirits and live? [10]For they indeed for a few days chastened us as seemed best

to them, but He for our profit, that we may be partakers of His holiness. [11]Now no chastening seems to be joyful for the present, but painful; nevertheless, afterward it yields the peaceable fruit of righteousness to those who have been trained by it.

81. I am drawing near with confidence
Hebrews 4:16—Let us therefore come boldly to the throne of grace that we may obtain mercy and find grace to help in time of need.

82. I am empowered to obey
Philippians2:13—for it is God who works in you both to will and to do for *His* good pleasure.

83. I am encouraged
2 Thessalonians 2:16-17—Now may our Lord Jesus Christ Himself, and our God and Father, who has loved us and given *us* everlasting consolation and good hope by grace, [17]comfort your hearts and establish you in every good word and work.

84. I am enlightened
Ephesians 1:18—the eyes of your understanding being enlightened; that you may know what is the hope of His calling, what are the riches of the glory of His inheritance in the saints,

85. I am enriched in everything

1 Corinthians 1:5—that you were enriched in everything by Him in all utterance and all knowledge

86. I am equipped

2 Timothy 3:16-17—All Scripture *is* given by inspiration of God, and *is* profitable for doctrine, for reproof, for correction, for instruction in righteousness, [17] that the man of God may be complete, thoroughly equipped for every good work.

87. I am established

Deuteronomy 28:9—"The LORD will establish you as a holy people to Himself, just as He has sworn to you, if you keep the commandments of the LORD your God and walk in His ways.

88. I have eternal life

John 3:36—He who believes in the Son has everlasting life; and he who does not believe the Son shall not see life, but the wrath of God abides on him."

89. I have every good thing

Philemon 6—that the sharing of your faith may become effective by the acknowledgment of every good thing which is in you in Christ Jesus.

90. I am exalted at His right hand

Acts 2: 34-35—"For David did not ascend into the heavens, but he says himself:

' *The LORD said to my Lord,*

" *Sit at My right hand,*

³⁵ *Till I make Your enemies Your footstool.*'"

91. I am faithful

Revelation 17:14—These will make war with the Lamb, and the Lamb will overcome them, for He is Lord of lords and King of kings; and those *who are* with Him *are* called, chosen, and faithful."

92. I am family

Psalm 68:5—A father of the fatherless, a defender of widows, *Is* God in His holy habitation.

93. I am far from oppression

Isaiah 54:14—In righteousness you shall be established; You shall be far from oppression, for you shall not fear; And from terror, for it shall not come near you.

94. I am favored

Job 10:12—You have granted me life and favor, And Your care has preserved my spirit.

95. I am a fellow citizen with the saints

Ephesians 2:19—Now, therefore, you are no

longer strangers and foreigners, but fellow citizens with the saints and members of the household of God,

96. I am a fellow worker
Colossians 4:11—and Jesus who is called Justus. These *are my* only fellow workers for the kingdom of God who are of the circumcision; they have proved to be a comfort to me.

97. I am filled
Act. 2:4—And they were all filled with the Holy Spirit and began to speak with other tongues, as the Spirit gave them utterance.

98. I am filled to the fullness of God
Colossians 2:9-10—For in Him dwells all the fullness of the Godhead bodily; [10] and you are complete in Him, who is the head of all principality and power.

99. I am filled with the fruit of righteousness
Philippians 1:11—being filled with the fruits of righteousness which *are* by Jesus Christ, to the glory and praise of God.

100. I am filled with the fruit of the Spirit
Galatians 5:22-23—But the fruit of the Spirit

is love, joy, peace, longsuffering, kindness, goodness, faithfulness, [23] gentleness, self-control. Against such there is no law.

101. I am filled with the knowledge of His will

Colossians 1:9—for this reason we also, since the day we heard it, do not cease to pray for you, and to ask that you may be filled with the knowledge of His will in all wisdom and spiritual understanding;

102. I am filled with joy

John 17:13—But now I come to You, and these things I speak in the world, that they may have My joy fulfilled in themselves.

103. I am a finished product in progress

Philippians 1:6—being confident of this very thing, that He who has begun a good work in you will complete *it* until the day of Jesus Christ;

104. I am a first fruit

Romans 8:23—Not only *that,* but we also who have the firstfruits of the Spirit, even we ourselves groan within ourselves, eagerly waiting for the adoption, the redemption of our body.

105. I am forgiven

Ephesians 1:7—In Him we have redemption

through His blood, the forgiveness of sins, according to the riches of His grace

106. I am formed in the womb by God

Jeremiah 1:5— "Before I formed you in the womb I knew you;
>Before you were born I sanctified you;
>I ordained you a prophet to the nations."

107. I was lost, but now I'm found

Luke 19:10—for the Son of Man has come to seek and to save that which was lost."

108. I am a fragrance

1 Corinthians 1:15-16—lest anyone should say that I had baptized in my own name. [16] Yes, I also baptized the household of Stephanas. Besides, I do not know whether I baptized any other.

109. I am free

John 8:36—Therefore if the Son makes you free, you shall be free indeed.

110. I am freely given all things

Romans 8:32—He who did not spare His own Son, but delivered Him up for us all, how shall He not with Him also freely give us all things?

111. I am gifted

Romans 12:6—Having then gifts differing according to the grace that is given to us, *let us use them:* if prophecy, *let us prophesy* in proportion to our faith;

112. I am given His magnificent promises
2 Peter 1:3-4 —as His divine power has given to us all things that *pertain* to life and godliness, through the knowledge of Him who called us by glory and virtue, ⁴ by which have been given to us exceedingly great and precious promises, that through these you may be partakers of the divine nature, having escaped the corruption *that is* in the world through lust.

113. I am given His Holy Spirit
2 Corinthians 1:22—who also has sealed us and given us the Spirit in our hearts as a guarantee.

114. I am glorified with Him
2 Thessalonians 2:14—to which He called you by our gospel, for the obtaining of the glory of our Lord Jesus Christ.

115. I am God's child
John 1:12—But as many as received Him, to them He gave the right to become children of God, to those who believe in His name:

116. I am God's gift to Christ

John 17:24—"Father, I desire that they also whom You gave Me may be with Me where I am, that they may behold My glory which You have given Me; for You loved Me before the foundation of the world.

117. I know God is for me

Romans 8:31—What then shall we say to these things? If God *is* for us, who *can be* against us?

118. I am gracious

Proverbs 22:11—He who loves purity of heart *and has* grace on his lips,

The king *will be* his friend.

119. I am granted grace in Christ Jesus

Romans 5:17,20—For if by the one man's offense death reigned through the one, much more those who receive abundance of grace and of the gift of righteousness will reign in life through the One, Jesus Christ.) [20] Moreover the law entered that the offense might abound. But where sin abounded, grace abounded much more,

120. I am guarded by God

2 Timothy 1:12—For this reason I also suffer these things; nevertheless I am not ashamed, for I know whom I have believed and am persuaded

that He is able to keep what I have committed to Him until that Day.

121. I am guarded by God's peace
Philippians 4:7—and the peace of God, which surpasses all understanding, will guard your hearts and minds through Christ Jesus.

122. I am guaranteed
Ephesians 1:13-14—In Him you also *trusted,* after you heard the word of truth, the gospel of your salvation; in whom also, having believed, you were sealed with the Holy Spirit of promise, [14] who is the guarantee of our inheritance until the redemption of the purchased possession, to the praise of His glory.

123. I am guided
Psalm 48:14—For this *is* God, Our God forever and ever; He will be our guide *even* to death.

124. I am guiltless
Romans 8:1—T*here is* therefore now no condemnation to those who are in Christ Jesus, who do not walk according to the flesh, but according to the Spirit.

125. I am the head
Deuteronomy 28:13—And the LORD will make you

the head and not the tail; you shall be above only, and not be beneath, if you heed the commandments of the LORD your God, which I command you today, and are careful to observe *them.*

126. I am healed
1 Peter 2:24—who Himself bore our sins in His own body on the tree, that we, having died to sins, might live for righteousness—by whose stripes you were healed.

127. I am healthy
Deuteronomy 7:15—And the LORD will take away from you all sickness, and will afflict you with none of the terrible diseases of Egypt which you have known, but will lay *them* on all those who hate you.

128. I am an heir of God
Titus 3:7—that having been justified by His grace we should become heirs according to the hope of eternal life.

129. I am helped by Him
Isaiah 44:2—Thus says the LORD who made you and formed you from the womb, *who* will help you:

130. I am hidden with Christ in God

Colossians 3:3—For you died, and your life is hidden with Christ in God.

131. I am His
Isaiah 43:1—But now, thus says the LORD, who created you, O Jacob,

And He who formed you, O Israel: " Fear not, for I have redeemed you;

I have called *you* by your name; You *are* Mine.

132. I am His handiwork
Ephesians 2:10—For we are His workmanship, created in Christ Jesus for good works, which God prepared beforehand that we should walk in them.

133. I am holy
Ephesians 1:4—just as He chose us in Him before the foundation of the world, that we should be holy and without blame before Him in love

134. I am honored
2 Timothy 2:21—Therefore if anyone cleanses himself from the latter, he will be a vessel for honor, sanctified and useful for the Master, prepared for every good work.

135. I am humble
Philippians 2:24—But I trust in the Lord that I

myself shall also come shortly.

136. I am the image of God
Genesis 1:27—So God created man in His *own* image; in the image of God He created him; male and female He created them.

137. I am the image and glory of God
1 Corinthians 11:7—For a man indeed ought not to cover *his* head, since he is the image and glory of God; but woman is the glory of man.

138. I am an imitator of God
Ephesians 5:1—Therefore be imitators of God as dear children.

139. I am in Christ Jesus
1 Corinthians 1:30—But of Him you are in Christ Jesus, who became for us wisdom from God—and righteousness and sanctification and redemption

140. I am included
Ephesians 1:13—In Him you also *trusted,* after you heard the word of truth, the gospel of your salvation; in whom also, having believed, you were sealed with the Holy Spirit of promise,

141. I am indestructible
John 6:51—I am the living bread which came

down from heaven. If anyone eats of this bread, he will live forever; and the bread that I shall give is My flesh, which I shall give for the life of the world."

142. I am indwelt by Christ Jesus
John 14:20 At that day you will know that I *am* in My Father, and you in Me, and I in you.

143. I am indwelt by His Spirit
Romans 8:11—But if the Spirit of Him who raised Jesus from the dead dwells in you, He who raised Christ from the dead will also give life to your mortal bodies through His Spirit who dwells in you.

144. I am inscribed on His palms
Isaiah 49:16—See, I have inscribed you on the palms *of My hands;*

Your walls *are* continually before Me.

145. I am inseparable from His love
Romans 8:35 Who shall separate us from the love of Christ? *Shall* tribulation, or distress, or persecution, or famine, or nakedness, or peril, or sword?

146. I am an instrument of righteousness
Roman 6:13—And do not present your members

as instruments of unrighteousness to sin, but present yourselves to God as being alive from the dead, and your members *as* instruments of righteousness to God.

147. I am joyful
Philippians 4:4—Rejoice in the Lord always. Again I will say, rejoice!

148. I am justified
Acts 13:39—and by Him everyone who believes is justified from all things from which you could not be justified by the law of Moses.

149. I am kept
Isaiah 38:17—Indeed *it was* for *my own* peace *That* I had great bitterness;
But You have lovingly *delivered* my soul from the pit of corruption,
For You have cast all my sins behind Your back.

150. I am in a Kingdom of priests
Revelation 1:6—and has made us kings and priests to His God and Father, to Him *be* glory and dominion forever and ever. Amen.

151. I am a King's kid
Psalm 44:4—You are my King, O God; Command victories for Jacob.

152. I know all things work together for good

Roman 8:28—And we know that all things work together for good to those who love God, to those who are the called according to *His* purpose.

153. I know Whom I believe

2 Timothy 1:12—For this reason I also suffer these things; nevertheless I am not ashamed, for I know whom I have believed and am persuaded that He is able to keep what I have committed to Him until that Day.

154. I am known

2 Timothy 2: 19—Nevertheless the solid foundation of God stands, having this seal: "The Lord knows those who are His," and, "Let everyone who names the name of Christ depart from iniquity."

155. I lack no wisdom

James 1:5—If any of you lacks wisdom, let him ask of God, who gives to all liberally and without reproach, and it will be given to him.

156. I am lavished with riches of His grace

Ephesians 1:7-8—In Him we have redemption through His blood, the forgiveness of sins, according to the riches of His grace [8] which He made to abound toward us in all wisdom and prudence,

157. I am led in Christ's triumph
2 Corinthians 2:14— Now thanks *be* to God who always leads us in triumph in Christ, and through us diffuses the fragrance of His knowledge in every place.

158. I am liberated
Romans 6:23—For the wages of sin *is* death, but the gift of God *is* eternal life in Christ Jesus our Lord.

159. I have life abundant
1 John 4:9— In this the love of God was manifested toward us, that God has sent His only begotten Son into the world, that we might live through Him.
John 10:10 The thief does not come except to steal, and to kill, and to destroy. I have come that they may have life, and that they may have *it* more abundantly.

160. I have life and peace in the Spirit
Romans 8:—6 For to be carnally minded *is* death, but to be spiritually minded *is* life and peace.

161. I have light

John 8:12—Then Jesus spoke to them again, saying, "I am the light of the world. He who follows Me shall not walk in darkness, but have the light of life."

162. I am a light in a dark place

Acts 13:47—For so the Lord has commanded us:
' *I have set you as a light to the Gentiles,*
That you should be for salvation to the ends
of the earth."

163. I have life flowing through me

John 7:38—He who believes in Me, as the Scripture has said, out of his heart will flow rivers of living water."

164. I am like a watered garden

Isaiah 58:11—The LORD will guide you continually,
And satisfy your soul in drought, And strengthen your bones;
You shall be like a watered garden,
And like a spring of water, whose waters do not fail.

165. I am a living stone in a spiritual house

1 Peter 2:5—you also, as living stones, are being built up a spiritual house, a holy priesthood, to offer up spiritual sacrifices acceptable to God through Jesus Christ.

166. I am the Lord's

Isaiah 44:5—One will say, 'I *am* the LORD's';
    Another will call *himself* by the name of Jacob;
    Another will write *with* his hand, 'The LORD's,'
    And name *himself* by the name of Israel.

167. I am loved

John 3:16—For God so loved the world that He gave His only begotten Son, that whoever believes in Him should not perish but have everlasting life.

168.I am loved constantly, unconditionally

Isaiah 43:4—Since you were precious in My sight,
 You have been honored, And I have loved you;
 Therefore I will give men for you, And people for your life.

169. I am loyal

Psalm 86:2—Preserve my life, for I *am* holy; You are my God;
Save Your servant who trusts in You!

170. I am made by Him

Psalm 100:3—Know that the LORD, He *is* God;
    It is He *who* has made us, and not we

ourselves;

We are His people and the sheep of His pasture.

171. I am a magnifier of God
Psalm 69:30—I will praise the name of God with a song,

And will magnify Him with thanksgiving.

172. I am marked
Ephesians 1:13—In Him you also *trusted,* after you heard the word of truth, the gospel of your salvation; in whom also, having believed, you were sealed with the Holy Spirit of promise.

173. I am a member of His body
Ephesians 5:30—For we are members of His body,[d] of His flesh and of His bones.

174. I am mighty in God
Luke 10:19—Behold, I give you the authority to trample on serpents and scorpions, and over all the power of the enemy, and nothing shall by any means hurt you.

175. I have the mind of Christ
1 Corinthians 2:16—For *"who has known the mind of the LORD that he may instruct Him?"* But we have the mind of Christ.

176. I am a minister

2 Corinthians 3:6—who also made us sufficient as ministers of the new covenant, not of the letter but of the Spirit;[a] for the letter kills, but the Spirit gives life.

177. I am a minister of reconciliation

2 Corinthians 5:18-19—Now all things *are* of God, who has reconciled us to Himself through Jesus Christ, and has given us the ministry of reconciliation, [19] that is, that God was in Christ reconciling the world to Himself, not imputing their trespasses to them, and has committed to us the word of reconciliation.

178. I am a mountain mover

Mark 11: 22-23—So Jesus answered and said to them, "Have faith in God. [23] For assuredly, I say to you, whoever says to this mountain, 'Be removed and be cast into the sea,' and does not doubt in his heart, but believes that those things he says will be done, he will have whatever he says.

179. I am named

Isaiah 43:1—But now, thus says the LORD, who created you, O Jacob,

And He who formed you, O Israel:

" Fear not, for I have redeemed you;

I have called *you* by your name;
You *are* Mine.

180. I am near to God
Ephesians 2:13—But now in Christ Jesus you who once were far off have been brought near by the blood of Christ.

181. I am never forsaken
Hebrew 13:5—Let your conduct be without covetousness; be content with such things as you have. For He Himself has said, "I will never leave you nor forsake you."

182. I am new
Ephesians 4:24—and that you put on the new man which was created according to God, in true righteousness and holiness.

183. I am new born
1 Peter 2:2—as newborn babes, desire the pure milk of the word that you may grow thereby

184. I am a new creation
2 Corinthians 5:17—Therefore, if anyone *is* in Christ, *he is* a new creation; old things have passed away; behold, all things have become new.

185. I have new life

Romans 6:4—Therefore we were buried with Him through baptism into death, that just as Christ was raised from the dead by the glory of the Father, even so we also should walk in newness of life.

186. I am part of a new race
1 Peter 2:9—But you *are* a chosen generation, a royal priesthood, a holy nation, His own special people, that you may proclaim the praises of Him who called you out of darkness into His marvelous light;

187. I am not condemned
Roman 8:1—T*here is* therefore now no condemnation to those who are in Christ Jesus,[a] who do not walk according to the flesh, but according to the Spirit

188. I am no longer a slave to sin
Roman 6:6—knowing this, that our old man was crucified with *Him* that the body of sin might be done away with, that we should no longer be slaves of sin.

189. I have not been given a spirit of fear
1 Timothy 1:7—desiring to be teachers of the law, understanding neither what they say nor the things which they affirm.

190. I am obedient

Isaiah 1:19—If you are willing and obedient,
    You shall eat the good of the land;
        [20] But if you refuse and rebel,
    You shall be devoured by the sword";
    For the mouth of the LORD has spoken.

191. I am an object of mercy

Romans 9:23—and that He might make known the riches of His glory on the vessels of mercy, which He had prepared beforehand for glory,

192. I am obtained an inheritance

Ephesians 1:11—In Him also we have obtained an inheritance, being predestined according to the purpose of Him who works all things according to the counsel of His will,

193. I am of God's household

Ephesians 2:19—Now, therefore, you are no longer strangers and foreigners, but fellow citizens with the saints and members of the household of God,

194. I am on the winning side

Colossians 2:15 Having disarmed principalities and powers, He made a public spectacle of them, triumphing over them in it.

195. I am one with Him

John 17:23-24—I in them, and You in Me; that they may be made perfect in one, and that the world may know that You have sent Me, and have loved them as You have loved Me.
24 "Father, I desire that they also whom You gave Me may be with Me where I am, that they may behold My glory which You have given Me; for You loved Me before the foundation of the world.

196. I am an over comer

1 John 5:4-5—For whatever is born of God overcomes the world. And this is the victory that has overcome the world—our[a] faith. 5 Who is he who overcomes the world, but he who believes that Jesus is the Son of God?

197. I am pardoned

Jeremiah33:8—I will cleanse them from all their iniquity by which they have sinned against Me, and I will pardon all their iniquities by which they have sinned and by which they have transgressed against Me.

198. I am a partaker of Christ

Hebrews 3:14—For we have become partakers of Christ if we hold the beginning of our confidence steadfast to the end,

199. I am a partaker of the Holy Spirit

Hebrews 6:4—For *it is* impossible for those who were once enlightened, and have tasted the heavenly gift, and have become partakers of the Holy Spirit,

200. I am a partaker of grace

Philippians 1:7—just as it is right for me to think this of you all, because I have you in my heart, inasmuch as both in my chains and in the defense and confirmation of the gospel, you all are partakers with me of grace.

201. I am a partaker of the promise in Christ

Ephesians 3:6—that the Gentiles should be fellow heirs, of the same body, and partakers of His promise in Christ through the gospel,

202. I have passed from death to life

John 5:24—"Most assuredly, I say to you, he who hears My word and believes in Him who sent Me has everlasting life, and shall not come into judgment, but has passed from death into life.

203 I am patient

James 5:8—You also be patient. Establish your hearts, for the coming of the Lord is at hand.

204. I have peace

Philippians 4:7—and the peace of God, which surpasses all understanding, will guard your hearts and minds through Christ Jesus.

205. I am one of the people of God

1 Peter 2:9—But you *are* a chosen generation, a royal priesthood, a holy nation, His own special people, that you may proclaim the praises of Him who called you out of darkness into His marvelous light;

206. I am being perfected

1 Peter 5:10—But may the God of all grace, who called us to His eternal glory by Christ Jesus, after you have suffered a while, perfect, establish, strengthen, and settle *you.*

207. I am pleasing to God

Psalm 149:4 For the LORD takes pleasure in His people;

He will beautify the humble with salvation.

208. I am God's own possession

Titus 2:14—who gave Himself for us, that He might redeem us from every lawless deed and purify for Himself *His* own special people, zealous for good works.

209. I am possessor of all things

1 Corinthians 3:21-23—Therefore let no one boast in men. For all things are yours: 22 whether Paul or Apollos or Cephas, or the world or life or death, or things present or things to come—all are yours. 23 And you *are* Christ's, and Christ *is* God's.

210. I have the power of God behind me

Philippians 3:21—who will transform our lowly body that it may be conformed to His glorious body, according to the working by which He is able even to subdue all things to Himself.

211. I have power

Acts 1:8—But you shall receive power when the Holy Spirit has come upon you; and you shall be witnesses to Me in Jerusalem, and in all Judea and Samaria, and to the end of the earth."

212. I have power over the devil

Luke 9:1—Then He called His twelve disciples together and gave them power and authority over all demons, and to cure diseases.

213. I am predestined

Ephesians 1:11—In Him also we have obtained an inheritance, being predestined according to the purpose of Him who works all things according to the counsel of His will,

214. I am prepared beforehand for glory

Romans 9:23—And *He did so* to make known the riches of His glory upon vessels of mercy, which He prepared beforehand for glory,

215. I am prosperous

Psalm 1:3—He shall be like a tree
>   Planted by the rivers of water,
>   That brings forth its fruit in its season,
>   Whose leaf also shall not wither;
>   And whatever he does shall prosper.

216. I am protected

Psalm 91:14—"Because he has set his love upon Me, therefore I will deliver him; I will set him on high, because he has known My name.

217. I am provided for

Matthew 6:33—But seek first the kingdom of God and His righteousness, and all these things shall be added to you.

218. I am purchased

Revelation 5:9—And they sang a new song, saying:
>   " You are worthy to take the scroll,
>   And to open its seals;
>   For You were slain,
>   And have redeemed us to God by Your blood
>   Out of every tribe and tongue and people and

nation,

219. I am purposeful
Psalm 138:8—The LORD will perfect *that which* concerns me;

> Your mercy, O LORD, *endures* forever;
> Do not forsake the works of Your hands.

220. I am qualified
Colossians 1:12—giving thanks to the Father who has qualified us to be partakers of the inheritance of the saints in the light.

221. I am raised up with Christ
Ephesians 2:6—and raised *us* up together, and made *us* sit together in the heavenly *places* in Christ Jesus,

222. I am ransomed with Him
Isaiah 35:10 And the ransomed of the LORD shall return,

> And come to Zion with singing,
> With everlasting joy on their heads.
> They shall obtain joy and gladness,
> And sorrow and sighing shall flee away.

223. I am rare
Proverbs 20:15—There is gold and a multitude of rubies,

But the lips of knowledge *are* a precious jewel.

224. I have received mercy
1 Peter 2:10—who once *were* not a people but *are* now the people of God, who had not obtained mercy but now have obtained mercy.

225. I have received an unshakable Kingdom
Hebrews 12:28 herefore, since we are receiving a kingdom which cannot be shaken, let us have grace, by which we may[i] serve God acceptably with reverence and godly fear.

226. I am reconciled to God
Romans 5:10—For if when we were enemies we were reconciled to God through the death of His Son, much more, having been reconciled, we shall be saved by His life.

227. I am redeemed
Galatians 3:13—Christ has redeemed us from the curse of the law, having become a curse for us (for it is written, *"Cursed is everyone who hangs on a tree"*),

228. I am refined
Isaiah 48:10—Behold, I have refined you, but not as silver;

I have tested you in the furnace of affliction.

229. I am reigning
Romans 5:17—For if by the one man's offense death reigned through the one, much more those who receive abundance of grace and of the gift of righteousness will reign in life through the One, Jesus Christ.

230. I am rejoicing
Romans 5:2-3—through whom also we have access by faith into this grace in which we stand, and rejoice in hope of the glory of God. 3 And not only *that,* but we also glory in tribulations, knowing that tribulation produces perseverance;

231. I am renewed
2 Corinthians 4:16—Therefore we do not lose heart. Even though our outward man is perishing, yet the inward *man* is being renewed day by day.

232. I am His representative
Matthew 5:16—Let your light so shine before men, that they may see your good works and glorify your Father in heaven.

233. I am rescued
Colossians 1:13—He has delivered us from the

power of darkness and conveyed *us* into the kingdom of the Son of His love,

234. I have rest provided
Matthew 11:28-30—Come to Me, all *you* who labor and are heavy laden, and I will give you rest. [29] Take My yoke upon you and learn from Me, for I am gentle and lowly in heart, and you will find rest for your souls. [30] For My yoke *is* easy and My burden is light.

235. I am rewarded by God
Isaiah 49:4—Then I said, 'I have labored in vain,
I have spent my strength for nothing and in vain;
Yet surely my just reward *is* with the LORD,
And my work with my God.'"

236. I am rich
2 Corinthians 8:9—For you know the grace of our Lord Jesus Christ, that though He was rich, yet for your sakes He became poor, that you through His poverty might become rich.

237. I am righteous
Ephesians 4:22—that you put off, concerning your former conduct, the old man which grows corrupt according to the deceitful lusts,

238. I am rooted an built up in Him

Colossians 2:7—rooted and built up in Him and established in the faith, as you have been taught, abounding in it[b] with thanksgiving.

239. I am royalty

Romans 5:17—For if by the one man's offense death reigned through the one, much more those who receive abundance of grace and of the gift of righteousness will reign in life through the One, Jesus Christ. 8:16-17—The Spirit Himself bears witness with our spirit that we are children of God, [17] and if children, then heirs—heirs of God and joint heirs with Christ, if indeed we suffer with *Him,* that we may also be glorified together.

240. I am a royal priesthood

1 Peter 2:9—But you *are* a chosen generation, a royal priesthood, a holy nation, His own special people, that you may proclaim the praises of Him who called you out of darkness into His marvelous light;

241. I am safe

Psalm 4:8—I will both lie down in peace, and sleep;

For You alone, O LORD, make me dwell in safety.

242. I am a saint of God

Psalm 34:9 Oh, fear the LORD, you His saints!

There is no want to those who fear Him.

243. I am the salt of the earth
Matthew 5:13— "You are the salt of the earth; but if the salt loses its flavor, how shall it be seasoned? It is then good for nothing but to be thrown out and trampled underfoot by men.

244. I am sanctified
1 Corinthians 6:11— And such were some of you. But you were washed, but you were sanctified, but you were justified in the name of the Lord Jesus and by the Spirit of our God.

245. I am satisfied
Jeremiah 31:14—I will satiate the soul of the priests with abundance,
And My people shall be satisfied with My goodness, says the LORD."

246. I am saved
Ephesians2:8— For by grace you have been saved through faith, and that not of yourselves; *it is* the gift of God,

247. I am sealed by God with His Holy Spirit,
Ephesians 1:13— In Him you also *trusted,* after you heard the word of truth, the gospel of your

salvation; in whom also, having believed, you were sealed with the Holy Spirit of promise,

248. I m seated with Him
Ephesians2:6, and raised *us* up together, and made *us* sit together in the heavenly *places* in Christ Jesus,

249. I am secure
Deuteronomy 33:12— Of Benjamin he said:
"The beloved of the LORD shall dwell in safety by Him,
Who shelters him all the day-long;
And he shall dwell between His shoulders."

250. I am sent
John 20:21—So Jesus said to them again, "Peace to you! As the Father has sent Me, I also send you."

251. I am set free
John 8:31-32,36— Then Jesus said to those Jews who believed Him, "If you abide in My word, you are My disciples indeed. 32 And you shall know the truth, and the truth shall make you free." 36. Therefore if the Son makes you free, you shall be free indeed.

252. I am sharing Christ's inheritance
Roman 8:17—It is also written in your law that

the testimony of two men is true.

253. I am sharing His glory
John 17:22—24 And the glory which You gave Me I have given them, that they may be one just as We are one: [24] "Father, I desire that they also whom You gave Me may be with Me where I am, that they may behold My glory which You have given Me; for You loved Me before the foundation of the world.

254. I am His sheep
Psalm 23:1— The LORD *is* my shepherd; I shall not want.

255. I am sheltered
Psalm 91:1—He who dwells in the secret place of the Most High shall abide under the shadow of the Almighty.

256. I am shield
Psalm 91:4—He shall cover you with His feathers,

> And under His wings you shall take refuge;
> His truth *shall be your* shield and buckler.

257. I am a slave to righteousness
Roman 6:18—And having been set free from sin, you became slaves of righteousness.

258. I am His soldier

2 Timothy 2:3-4—You therefore must endure[a] hardship as a good soldier of Jesus Christ. 4 No one engaged in warfare entangles himself with the affairs of *this* life, that he may please him who enlisted him as a soldier.

259. I am a son of God

Roman 8:14— For as many as are led by the Spirit of God, these are sons of God.

260. I am stable

Isaiah 33:6—Wisdom and knowledge will be the stability of your times,

And the strength of salvation;
The fear of the LORD *is* His treasure.

261. I am standing in His grace,

Romans 5:2— through whom also we have access by faith into this grace in which we stand, and rejoice in hope of the glory of God.

262. I am standing firm in Christ

2 Corinthians 1:21— Now He who establishes us with you in Christ and has anointed us *is* God,

263. I have my steps established by the Lord

Psalm 37:23— The steps of a *good* man are ordered by the LORD,

And He delights in his way.

264. I am strengthened in Him
Ephesians 3:16— that He would grant you, according to the riches of His glory, to be strengthened with might through His Spirit in the inner man,

265. I am strong in the Lord
1 Corinthians 1:8—who will also confirm you to the end, *that you may be* blameless in the day of our Lord Jesus Christ

266. I am amply supplied
Philippians 4:18—Indeed I have all and abound. I am full, having received from Epaphroditus the things *sent* from you, a sweet-smelling aroma, an acceptable sacrifice, well pleasing to God.

267. I am sustained from birth
Psalm 71:6—By You I have been upheld from birth;
You are He who took me out of my mother's womb.
My praise *shall be* continually of You.

268. I am a temple
1 Corinthians 3:16—Do you not know that you are the temple of God and *that* the Spirit of God dwells in you?

269. I am thought about
Psalm 139:17-18—How precious also are Your thoughts to me, O God! How great is the sum of them! ¹⁸*If* I should count them, they would be more in number than the sand; When I awake, I am still with You.

270. I am transferred into His Kingdom
Colossians 1:13—He has delivered us from the power of darkness and conveyed *us* into the kingdom of the Son of His love,

271. I am transformed
2 Corinthians 3:18—But we all, with unveiled face, beholding as in a mirror the glory of the Lord, are being transformed into the same image from glory to glory, just as by the Spirit of the Lord.

272. I am treasured
Psalm 83:3—They lay crafty plans against your people; they consult together against your **treasured** ones. (NIV)

273. I am triumphant
2 Corinthians 2:14—Now thanks *be* to God who always leads us in triumph in Christ, and through us diffuses the fragrance of His knowledge in every place.

274. I am unafraid

Isaiah 44:2—Thus says the LORD who made you
And formed you from the womb, *who* will
help you:
'Fear not, O Jacob My servant;
And you, Jeshurun, whom I have chosen.
51:12—" I, *even* I, *am* He who comforts you.
Who *are* you that you should be afraid
Of a man *who* will die,
And of the son of a man *who* will be made
like grass?

275. I am understood

Ephesians 1:8—which He made to abound toward
us in all wisdom and prudence,

276. I am united with Christ

Romans 6:5—For if we have been united together
in the likeness of His death, certainly we also
shall be *in the likeness* of *His* resurrection,

277. I am upheld

Psalm 37:17—For the arms of the wicked shall be
broken, But the LORD upholds the righteous.

278. I am upright

Psalm 7:10—My defense *is* of God, Who saves
the upright in heart.

279. I am unblemished

Colossians 1:22—in the body of His flesh through death, to present you holy, and blameless, and above reproach in His sight—

280. I have understanding

2 Timothy 2:7—Consider what I say, and may[b] the Lord give you understanding in all things.

281. I am useful for His glory

Isaiah 43:7—Everyone who is called by My name,
Whom I have created for My glory;
I have formed him, yes, I have made him."

282. I am valuable

Luke 12:24—Consider the ravens, for they neither sow nor reap, which have neither storehouse nor barn; and God feeds them. Of how much more value are you than the birds?

283. I live in victory

1 Corinthians 15:57—But thanks *be* to God, who gives us the victory through our Lord Jesus Christ.

284. I am walking in His light

1 John 1:7 But if we walk in the light as He is in the light, we have fellowship with one another, and the blood of Jesus Christ His Son cleanses us from all sin.

285. I am a warrior

2 Corinthians 10:4 For the weapons of our warfare *are* not carnal but mighty in God for pulling down strongholds,

286. I am washed

Titus 3:5 not by works of righteousness which we have done, but according to His mercy He saved us, through the washing of regeneration and renewing of the Holy Spirit,

287. I am watching for His return

Luke 12:37—Blessed *are* those servants whom the master, when he comes, will find watching. Assuredly, I say to you that he will gird himself and have them sit down *to eat,* and will come and serve them.

288. I am weak, then I am strong

2 Corinthians 12:10—Therefore I take pleasure in infirmities, in reproaches, in needs, in persecutions, in distresses, for Christ's sake. For when I am weak, then I am strong.

289. I am in a wealthy place

Psalm 66:12—You have caused men to ride over our heads;

> We went through fire and through water;
> But You brought us out to rich *fulfillment.*

290. I am welcome
Luke 11:9—"So I say to you, ask, and it will be given to you; seek, and you will find; knock, and it will be opened to you.

291. I am being made whole
Mark 5:34—And He said to her, "Daughter, your faith has made you well. Go in peace, and be healed of your affliction."

292. I put on the whole armor of God
Ephesians 6:11—Put on the whole armor of God, that you may be able to stand against the wiles of the devil.

293. I am wise
Proverbs 2:6 For the LORD gives wisdom; From His mouth *come* knowledge and understanding;

294. I am His witness
Acts 1:8—But you shall receive power when the Holy Spirit has come upon you; and you shall be witnesses to Me[a] in Jerusalem, and in all Judea and Samaria, and to the end of the earth."

295. I am His workmanship
Ephesians 2:10—For we are His workmanship, created in Christ Jesus for good works, which God

prepared beforehand that we should walk in them.

296. I am not of this world
John 17:14—I have given them Your word; and the world has hated them because they are not of the world, just as I am not of the world.

297. I am His worshipper
Psalm 95:6—Oh come, let us worship and bow down;
Let us kneel before the LORD our Maker.

298. I am worthy
Revelations 3:4—You have a few names even in Sardis who have not defiled their garments; and they shall walk with Me in white, for they are worthy.

299. I am yielded to God
Romans 6:13—And do not present your members *as* instruments of unrighteousness to sin, but present yourselves to God as being alive from the dead, and your members *as* instruments of righteousness to God.

300. I am yoked with Jesus
Matthew 11:29—Take My yoke upon you and learn from Me, for I am gentle and lowly in heart, and you will find rest for your soul